The Voice of
Sarah

The Voice of
Sarah

FEMININE SPIRITUALITY AND
TRADITIONAL JUDAISM

Tamar Frankiel

HarperSanFrancisco

A Division of HarperCollinsPublishers

FIRST EDITION

Library of Congress Cataloging-in-Publication Data

Frankiel, Tamar, 1946–
    The voice of Sarah : feminine spirituality and traditional Judaism / Tamar Frankiel.
        p.   cm.
    ISBN 0–06–063016–7
    1. Women in Judaism.   2. Women, Jewish—Religious life.
3. Feminism—Religious aspects—Judaism.   4. Orthodox Judaism––United States.   I. Title.
BM729.W6F73   1990
296'.082—dc20   90-4389
                                                                        CIP

90 91 92 93 94 HAD 10 9 8 7 6 5 4 3 2 1

This edition is printed on acid-free paper that meets the American National Standards Institute Z39.48 Standard.

TO MY CHILDREN

Shmuel Moshe

Yaakov Asher

Chana Chava

Rina Zipporah Chaya

and

Devorah Rachel

Your coming into the world
taught me about being
a Jewish woman.

Contents

"And God said to Abraham, . . . 'In everything that Sarah tells you, listen to her voice . . .'"

(GENESIS 21:12).

"And his mother [Rebecca] said to him [Jacob], 'Only listen to my voice . . .'"

(GENESIS 27:13)

Preface

This book has grown out of my experience and learning as an observant Jewish woman and as a feminist. Many women view these two categories as mutually exclusive. I once thought so too, but I now enjoy the struggle of living in both camps.

Many years ago I was a single, career-oriented feminist who happened to get interested in Jewish practice. As my involvement grew, I found myself attracted to orthodoxy in several ways. Shabbat was the first and most powerful attraction; then the richness, fervor, and individuality of traditional prayer services. Yet as I sat behind the *mechitza* that separates men and women, I raged at the limitations of "woman's place."

The attraction continued but the rage dwindled as I began to get acquainted with orthodox women. I found utterly incomprehensible their rationale for accepting this ancient way of life, but I saw that they were sincere. Moreover, I saw that they were, indisputably, powerful and influential in their families and communities. As I grew to know them, my first feelings of condescending pity toward these victims of patriarchy changed to admiration and wonderment. I knew *I* could never live like that, but I appreciated that they were living a life of integrity, with a spiritual richness of its own.

That was ten years ago. Today I find myself speaking in much the same way to others as those women spoke to me then: "I don't feel a need to be called to the Torah." "I have so many mitzvot to do myself, I don't think about doing men's mitzvot." "Raising Jewish children is one of the most satisfying and challenging things a person can do." I don't expect such statements to be any more believable to feminists than they were to me ten years ago. I can only assert that there is truth behind their simplicity.

At the same time, as an intellectual involved in the study of religion for nearly twenty-five years, I carry around other, more complex thoughts that support both my feminism and my Jewish practice. I have needed to think many things through in my own way, because it has often been easier for me to take on a practice than to accept the traditional reasons for it. For example, I couldn't accept laws about separation of men and women, or the emphasis on modesty in dress and behavior, simply because men needed protection from their own lustful thoughts. I didn't believe that women "didn't need as many mitzvot" or didn't need to pray with others because we were "more spiritual" than men—especially when I was also being told that we were so sensual that men were helpless in the face of female distractions.

As a feminist, if I had only been listening to the words, I wouldn't have stayed around for more than a few weeks. But I was also *doing* Judaism, and that was more powerful than anything I was told about it. And there was the continual evidence of the deep inner strength of the women around me. I couldn't believe that women like this would have lived for three thousand years under an oppressive male system that offered them nothing. No matter how strongly they believed that God gave the Torah and told them to do all these things, they could not have emerged so healthy, so whole as women unless the system were nourishing them.

I began looking for my own reasons for the Jewish woman's way of life, my own understanding of why I found it so powerful and how it had sustained millions of us for all these centuries. One can say, of course, that the ultimate reason is God, who has always sustained us in our spiritual as well as our physical life. That is undoubtedly so. But human beings were created in accord with God's plan for the whole universe, with its foundation in the Torah and its commandments, so that we would in fact be nourished by the religious actions we perform. I wanted to understand this. So I began drawing on my own reading in Judaism, and also on my years of studying comparative religion, to develop a deeper understanding of our tradition of feminine spirituality.

I found myself somewhat disappointed with the existing literature. On the one hand, most Jewish feminists were, understandably, struggling with the *halacha*, traditional Jewish law, which they perceived as unjust or inapplicable to the lives of modern women. Sometimes their arguments were excellent; but, whether I agreed or disagreed on any particular issue, I was not finding much help in understanding why this ancient practice was so powerful for me. On the other hand, explanations from orthodox rabbis or other observant writers at first seemed wooden or contrived. Interesting as this literature was, only occasionally would some fragment speak to me.

Still, there were bits and pieces, and it is these that I have finally begun to put together with the encouragement of my students and friends. In our spiritual education, there are fragments that come to us unexpectedly, often after much struggle, so that we seem to be hearing from outside what we already know inside. As the Torah says in a beloved passage in the book of D'varim (30:11–14), when Moshe exhorts the people,

This mandate that I am prescribing to you today is not too mysterious or remote from you. It is not in heaven, so [that you should] say, "Who shall go up to heaven and bring it to us so that we can hear it and keep it?" It is not over the sea so [that you should] say, "Who will cross the sea and get it for us, so that we will be able to hear it and keep it?" It is something that is very close to you. It is in your mouth and in your heart, so that you can keep it. (Deut. 30:11–14)

The Torah does speak to us, sometimes loudly, sometimes softly. I was finding that with the teachings as well as the practice, when I began really living it and seeking inside Torah, it was as if my own heart was speaking to me.

Now the work is to turn this outward, to speak out with my own voice about my experience and my understanding of it. This, to me, is at the essence of femininism, and I am still a feminist. I am also a scholar of comparative religion, and I occasionally draw on insights from that area of study. This sometimes makes what I have to say somewhat "unorthodox"; for we are taught that the Torah contains everything, and it can be dangerous to draw on teachings from non-Jewish traditions. Yet I would be denying an important part of myself if I did not bring what I know has enriched my experience and understanding of my own Jewish practice.

My intention is to stand firmly within the bounds of generally accepted halacha. I write in the spirit of Rabbi Nachman of Breslov's teaching: "You may expound the Torah and innovate in any area you wish. The only condition is that you may not use your interpretations to innovate or change any law."[1] Thus, despite my sympathy for feminism and my wide exposure to the secular wisdom of our time, I cannot join the chorus of voices who demand changes across the board in Jewish practice. I have come to know this Torah, this law, from another side. I know it has a beauty and depth that is at once strong and delicate, like a silken web. It cannot be tampered with carelessly and unknowingly, from the outside. Some of the very things that some feminists want to eliminate are sources of great spiritual growth for women. Certainly for me, deepening my commitment to Jewish practice has intensified my feminine consciousness in more ways than I can explain.

And yet I also sympathize with the bitter pain of many women who feel cheated by the tradition, who grew to adulthood feeling like second-class citizens, not having been given the resources of strength, courage, and self-esteem that should be every Jewish woman's birthright. For this to have happened, some grave deficiencies had developed in the passing on of the tradition to "the house of Jacob," that is, to the women. We must work with this pain and repair the flaws at their source.

This repair is not possible simply by giving women the same kind of recognition previously given only to men. There is no doubt we could do that; women have proven that with their intelligence, skills, and determination they can conquer any field. But we should ask, are we really doing ourselves a service by molding ourselves to these roles?

It is a little like asking a feminist in the peace movement if she believes women should be drafted to fight in the front lines. As a feminist, she may think she has to say yes. But her convictions tell her the whole enterprise of war is corrupt. Similarly, a religious feminist is caught between two principles. On the one hand is the demand for justice that is at the heart of Judaism and that points in the direction of egalitarianism. Perhaps we should restructure Judaism in the image of modern democratic society. But we know also that some aspects of that system are flawed: Can we in good conscience submit our spiritual tradition to the dictates of modern culture?

We must recognize also that the masculine-feminine structure of life is deeply embedded in the Jewish way of life. To what extent might the changes we invent undermine the power of the whole system? Is it possible that we might in fact be cutting ourselves off from the most direct way to a rich experience of God? It could be true, after all, that this Torah is "in your mouth and in your heart, so that you can keep it."

The path is not always clear for us today. We face more difficulties and complexities than most of the generations who came before us. We have in our communities more single women and divorced women than ever before. Many of us have careers and advanced educations that have enriched our experience of the world. All these make the traditional path look simplistic, obsolete, and presumably unsatisfying for sophisticated women. Yet I have found that the depths of history and experience that constitute what we know as Judaism are a reservoir of spiritual strength, which is exactly what I need most. I am writing this book to share my understanding of how this can be so: that this ancient wisdom and practice can fulfill our highest aspirations as well as our deepest desires.

I should note that my approach is different from that of many other contemporary writers. While I am well aware of biblical criticism, I have chosen not to draw on that resource here. Nor have I considered all the literature and commentary on women that exists in the tradition. Other writers have uncovered what they consider evidence of misogyny or patriarchal oppression in Judaism, and I am not disputing its existence. Instead, I have tried to present traditional Judaism as it has come to me, as a living teaching, with rich resources for my self-understanding as a woman. I have also tried to present material from highly accessible sources, all in English, so that others can easily follow up on my explorations.

I hope that my efforts will encourage other women who have thus far been silent to speak out, and that this work will become part of an ongoing dialogue of women from all branches of our tradition. We need to listen carefully to one another's voices and ensure that men listen as well. Together we can share the work of creating a Jewish life in our modern world, knowing that living Jewishly as a woman today is not without its difficulties, but it has its own hidden delights.

I want to acknowledge all the help I have received in coming to this work of writing. In the book, of course, any errors in fact or interpretation are my responsibility, and my statements do not represent the views of any person or group other than myself. But I do want to thank those, named or unnamed, who have helped me. May they receive merit from all that is good in this book and no blame for any of its faults. Many have taught and encouraged me along the way: I want to mention especially my husband, Hirsh Frankiel; Rabbi Chaim Dalfin and Basya Dalfin; Rabbi Yisroel Rice; and Rabbi Chaim Citron. My students have been receptive, responsive, and stimulating as well: thanks particularly to Marilee Stark, Helene Dano, Faye Zimmerman, and Barbara Corinblitt. My friends and family have been encouraging at many important points; I especially appreciate my husband's growing toleration for my compulsion to write, and the dedication expresses some part of my debt to my children. Thanks also to Suzanne Sadowsky and John Loudon who helped launch this book and to my religious community for their warmth and caring for me and my family.

This does not begin to exhaust the list of credits. But a few more special thanks: first, to Estelle Frankel who first opened me to the richness of midrash and, by her own spiritual aliveness, awakened my heart. The memory of sitting and listening to her teaching stays with me as an ongoing inspiration. Second, to Barbara Shindell, who taught me to hear and trust my own inner voices. Last but not least, to Jane Falk: without her support, encouragement, and critical reflection as my friend and colleague, I might never have been able to speak in a book such as this, in my own voice.

Part 1

HEARING FROM OUR PAST

As women of twentieth-century Western culture, we have found ourselves in an unprecedented situation. Thanks to technology, medicine, and cultural and economic changes, we have a degree of freedom, and a multiplicity of opportunities, that were unimaginable to women in earlier eras. Yet we do not always have the guidance we need to shape our new lives. Few of us can follow the patterns of our grandmothers; but our culture offers us few positive models as alternatives.

As a result, our search for a satisfying way of being in the world has turned us inward. Of necessity we have become psychologically oriented —with or without the help of therapists—in order to discover or create our own inner resources. In this inner work many women have turned to mythical archetypes—the female figures of myth, legend, and traditional history—as guideposts to understanding their feelings, experiences, and development as women. In my view, this is an important and fruitful path for building our self-esteem and shaping our development.

But explorations of feminine psychology in the search for models have most often led to the goddesses of Greek mythology, whom we in the West know best from classical tradition, or occasionally to non-Western figures like female bodhisattvas of China or goddess figures of India. This is not always satisfying to Jewish women. Why is it that our attention has not been directed to our own tradition, where we have stories of great women who have served as inspiration in previous ages? The reasons are multiple. First, we have largely accepted the Christian and post-Christian condemnation of Judaism as a "patriarchal" religion, indeed as the origin of Western "patriarchal consciousness" which is the source of male-dominated culture, oppressive to women. This assessment of Judaism is incorrect, as we will see later on. But even if one goes past cultural preconceptions, it often seems that the stories of Sarah, Rivkah (Rebecca), Rachel, Leah, and the others are so embedded in the stories of men or of events relevant to the whole Jewish people that the women seem to be simply helpmates, accessories to history. Further, the major figures have been extolled for their virtues as "the mothers": What relevance would they have to women seeking models beyond or in addition to motherhood?

But first impressions do not tell the whole story. The past does not belong only to men. As Elisabeth Schüssler Fiorenza has pointed out, we can, by "rereading the available sources in a different key," recover feminine dimensions in our stories and traditions.[1] Many women have begun to create modern "midrash" out of biblical women's stories. In my view we have not yet read carefully enough in the Torah, other biblical writings, and the midrash we already have. Even though the writers or compilers of this literature have been male, so far as we know, they often took account of the women in their stories as acting independently and having their own special character distinct from their husbands.

In this section we will take a new look at some of the portraits we have inherited of famous women of our tradition, in and for themselves. We will, I think, emerge with a quite different picture of these women: they represent neither appendages to their husbands nor some kind of "Jewish mother" stereotype. For me they appear now in a wondrous light: multidimensional and thus more real than the pagan goddesses, yet also great in their feminine spiritual achievements. Precisely because of their earthly reality, they function more clearly as spiritual beacons. Sarah and the other mothers, Tamar, Ruth, Yehudit, Channah, and others can become rich resources of inner guidance. In the sections that follow, I will try to describe how this is so.

CHAPTER 1

Voices of the Mothers

Sarah,
noblewoman,
why did you leave your homeland
to become his princess, Sarai?
What did you know,
what did you see ahead,
you who saw the destiny of our people?
Iscah,
prophetess,
you saw us before you,
your daughters,
lost in a land yet farther away.
Speak to us from Machpelah,
comfort us in our struggles,
laugh with us
that we may share the joy
of the impossible.

The women we call our "Mothers"—Sarah, Rivkah (Rebecca), Rachel, and Leah—are not merely mothers, any more than the "Fathers"—Abraham, Isaac, and Jacob—are merely fathers. We sometimes think of the women as absorbed with the problems of bearing children, for three of them experienced long periods of childlessness, and only one, Leah, bore more than two children (Gen. 11:30, 25:21, 29:31).

But, as a moment's thought will show, that in itself means they were not always preoccupied with the activities of motherhood—they spent many years without children. Today's stereotype of the mother who has a baby every year and talks of nothing but her children's activities is not what the Torah tells us about our collective mothers.[1] The idea of motherhood in Judaism is something else: it is the essence of womanhood, of the feminine side of our beings. It need not imply the physical fact of becoming a mother, bearing and nurturing a child, although for most women that experience is a significant spiritual opening. Rather, motherhood signifies a deep and profound inner connection to the future, to the acts and circumstances of today and their effect on the development of future generations. As mothers are bonded, physically and then emotionally, to their birth-children, so the mother in Jewish tradition is a person whose being is deeply involved, from the inside, with those who will come after.

The woman's intense concern with preparing for the future is connected with another feature of our mothers: their prophetic ability, the skill of foretelling the future. Tradition identifies seven biblical women, including Sarah, as possessing this ability to the extent that they were actually called prophetesses; and most commentators agree that Rivkah, Rachel, and Leah had some degree of the art as well. Prophecy is naturally connected with the woman's bond to the future: she *must* be able to see from today what will be tomorrow's consequences, not merely in a cause-and-effect way, as male logic would dictate, but as a sensed or felt gestalt. This is related to what we call "woman's intuition," an inner knowledge, or ability to read a situation and produce an insight into character.

These two aspects of the "mother" are connected with a third: her active exercise of power in the family. While biblical women did not generally exert political influence, for example by negotiating with outsiders or waging war (Devorah, a judge and prophet, was an exception), they exercised enormous power among their kin. Some have even suggested that Sarah, Rivkah, Rachel, and Leah came from a matriarchal society. This is not necessarily the case. It is more likely that Jewish society, in its origin, was more balanced than we are accustomed to think, given our conditioned perception of that society as "patriarchal."[2] Clearly, women effected significant changes in the destiny of the whole Jewish people by combining their prophetic ability with their power in the family.

The first mother, Sarah, reveals many dimensions of this maternal archetype. This woman, who had no children for ninety years, the wife of a respected chieftain and equal to him in rank, did not spend her time milking the goats or mending tent covers. The midrash tells us that, on the contrary, she worked as what we would today call a women's spiritual leader: she taught women about the one God, while Abraham taught the men. The great insight that resulted in the overthrow of paganism was his, but her work was equally important. She was so successful at drawing people to her that, when they worked in a new location, Abraham set up her tent first (Bereishis Rabba, Gen 12:8). She was a "mother" of souls.

The stories of Sarah provide a number of examples hinting at her character as a spiritually powerful person. She demonstrated her powers, for example, when she and Abraham went down to Egypt. Pharoah, after taking Sarah into his house as his consort, found himself stricken by a plague that affected even his genitals; he could not have relations with her without extreme pain. The text says, "The Lord plagued Pharaoh with great plagues, and his house, because of Sarai Abram's wife." Rashi, the great eleventh-century commentator on Bible and Talmud, points out that the phrase al-d'var Sarai, "because of Sarai," literally means "by the word of Sarai": "She tells the angel, 'Smite!' and he smites" (Gen. 12:17). She was a woman so connected to God that she could command the powers above.

Moreover, Sarah was a prophetess in her own right – greater, tradition tells us, than Abraham. She told him to take Hagar, her Egyptian serving maid, as a concubine, and "Abram hearkened to the voice of Sarai." The midrash comments that he listened to the Holy Spirit within her. Later, when she asked him to banish Hagar and her son Ishmael, Abraham hesitated. But God told him in no uncertain terms, "All that Sarah says to you, listen to her voice" (Gen. 21:12). This is, indeed, a piece of advice often given by rabbis to husbands down through the ages; for women are regarded as having a greater degree of insight in many circumstances. Rashi teaches from this that Abraham was inferior to Sarah in prophecy. She foresaw that the presence of Hagar's son would be dangerous to the future of the family, so he and his mother had to be separated from Isaac.

Sarah, in short, was by no means merely an appendage to Abraham. The lore about her portrays a woman of power. Had it not been for Sarah, our famous ancestors might have ended up slaves in Egypt a little too early. Yet she showed no fear of Pharaoh or the Egyptians, trusting in the protection of God. Had it not been for her, Abraham might have neglected Isaac in favor of Ishmael – indeed, he begged God to favor Ishmael; but God refused, insisting that he would have a son by Sarah to carry on the covenant. Sarah saw this clearly and acted decisively, while remaining part of a fruitful partnership.

Yet often the most revealing incidents relate not only a person's strengths or positive features, but also their tests or moments of weakness. Since what we seek most of all are models of spiritual development, this is especially important: How do these archetypal stories give us clues to our own inner work? Fortunately, the Torah is not mere eulogy. Not everything written about the patriarchs and matriarchs is entirely favorable, and that is true of Sarah as well.

One of the more curious passages in Bereishit (Genesis) has to do with Sarah's laughter at the prophecy that she would bear a son when she was ninety years old. When three angels in human disguise visited Abraham to tell him the prophecy, Sarah was standing in the door of the tent and overheard. (She was intended to hear, because one of the visitors had already asked her whereabouts and was told that she was in the tent.) On hearing the angel's words, she "laughed within herself, saying, 'After I am grown old, shall I have pleasure, my lord being old [also]?'" God spoke to Abraham about Sarah's laughter: "Is anything too hard for the Lord? . . . Sarah will have a son." Sarah then denied having laughed, and God—or, in some interpretations, Abraham—scolded her: "No, you laughed" (Gen. 18:12–15).

This apparently simple scene is actually quite complex. It seems a case of her laughing spontaneously at what seemed a ridiculous idea, then, on being confronted with it, recognizing that she had been laughing at God.[3] At a moment when she should have been serious and humble, she giggled; embarrassed, she denied having laughed. But if this were the end of the story, it would be rather simplistic. What is the point of telling us about Sarah's laughter?

Abraham had earlier laughed at the same news. After Ishmael's birth from Hagar, God appeared to him, changed his and Sarai's names, commanded circumcision, and promised that Sarah would bear a son. "Then Abraham fell upon his face and laughed, and said in his heart: 'To one of a hundred years old shall [a child] be born, or shall Sarah, ninety years old, bear?" (Gen. 17:17). Although he seems to have laughed for the same reason as Sarah, Abraham was not scolded for his laughter. Rashi, interpreting Onkelos's translation, comments that "Abraham believed and rejoiced, but Sarah did not believe, and sneered."[4] Rashi makes it sound worse than an accidental giggle that caused embarrassment: Sarah was ridiculing the prophecy. Yet the midrash tells us that Sarah did not know this was a prophecy.[5]

The third occasion for speaking of laughter is at Isaac's birth. His name, *Yitzchak* in Hebrew, comes from the root for "laugh." Sarah comments on his birth, "Laughter God has made for me; everyone that hears will laugh for me. . . . Who would have said to Abraham, Sarah would suckle children? But I have born a son in his old age" (Gen. 21:6–7). Now, Sarah herself makes clear that the laughter is clearly an expression of joy. But why was Sarah's laughter not reckoned that way before as Abraham's was? Why was she scolded for laughing?

One could argue that the passage where Sarah is scolded presents a negative view of a woman: she was not allowed to express herself like a man. Rashi's comments could be interpreted this way. But the story goes on to say that Sarah herself denied her laughter. Was she simply bowing to social pressure out of her embarrassment? No. Sarah, at the announcement of the prophecy, faced a moment of uncertainty. A moment of surprised delight was mixed with skepticism. She could neither fully believe nor affirm her disbelief. The spark of joy was veiled by fear—this might not be true—and it seems so impossible as to be awesome.

Not until the miracle of Isaac's birth—not until she knew fully from her own experience, did Sarah fully express her joy. Not until then could she proclaim her faith in her own way: everyone will laugh with me! All the stories indicate that she had been Abraham's partner all along in his new religious perspective. She taught about the one God; she knew how to command spiritual powers. But her earlier laughter hinted at a potential weakness, a residue of skepticism or, at least, an inability to affirm her own experience of God.

The birth of a child from her own body was for her an opening to a new level. It was the absolute assurance that her God, the God who gave her and her husband foresight and skill and who led them this far, really worked far beyond the bounds of human understanding, and worked in this world, not just in the spiritual realm. As Ellen Umansky has suggested, it was the sealing of God's "covenant" with Sarah, as circumcision had sealed his covenant with Abraham.[6] Abraham had come to understand through his visionary experiences. God had lifted him up above the stars, showing him that his destiny was above what fate or astrology might predict. Sarah experienced the direct physical manifestation of God's work in their lives, her skepticism turning to pure joy at the birth of a child. This was also the clear establishment of the covenant in connection with the maternal line. Circumcision was for Ishmael as well as Isaac; but the birth of Isaac represented a decision in favor of Sarah over Hagar.

The midrash comments in addition that when Isaac was born, many childless women also found themselves with child, many were healed, and many prayers answered with her, so there was great joy in the whole world. "Everyone will laugh," exclaimed Sarah—and those who will laugh with her includes us. Sarah's example teaches us that faith is not only a matter of serious, dedicated commitment, tests and trials like those of Abraham. If it were, we would be always vulnerable to a debilitating skepticism. Faith is connected with the experience of deep joy, in our real-life, here-and-now existence. Sarah experienced the fulfillment of God's will, over and above what she could possibly have predicted or dared to wish for, manifest not only in God's great plan for the future of the world, but in her personal life. This is the epitome of the experience of motherhood: the amazed, joyful realization that God has brought new life, through me! This is the grounding, certain aspect of faith.

Sarah, then, was a prophet, a woman of power and confidence, a voice to whom women, men, and angels listened. So far as we can tell, she was this kind of remarkable person all her life. Yet in her old age she experienced something new—a power beyond her imagining and beyond her keen sight. Her growth was in a deepening of faith, an opening to what she had believed impossible, and a new experience of joy. We can see reflected here two great emphases of Jewish teaching: that we must continually cultivate our faith, and that we should do everything *b'simcha*, with joy. We would all wish for ourselves such an epitaph as we have for Sarah: everyone will laugh with me! And we can all pray for Sarah's deeper faith that led her to the fulfillment of an impossible dream.

Sarah's story is not complete: a beginning acquaintance makes us want to know more about her. But we have reason to be especially grateful for these glimpses of her in Torah and midrash.[7] In other Mediterranean cultures in the period before 600 B.C.E., very few stories of women were preserved at all—goddesses, yes, or an occasional queen, but the human actors among legendary ancestors were almost all men. No one would have taken much notice if the wives of our forefathers had been left out of the picture entirely. But, rather than relegating them to the background, women are presented prominently in the so-called patriarchal tradition. Sarah, her voice speaking prophecy and laughing joyfully, is the foundation. Her edifice is "built up," as she would wish, in the words and actions of the women who follow.

Rivkah, Rachel, and Leah,
what are your blessings?
Rivkah, woman of destiny,
you would take destiny in your own hands!
Rachel, woman beloved,
your weeping on the road will bring us home.
Leah, woman of mystery eyes,
the world beyond is yours.
Inside us you live on.
We forge our lives from immalleable iron,
we weep,
we live twice-born.

The Torah and midrash suggest that Rivkah was made in the image of Sarah. The biblical text records that Abraham sent his servant Eliezer back to his homeland to acquire a wife for his son, Isaac, whereupon a remarkable "coincidence" occurred: the first woman Eliezer met happened to be not only a woman of good character, but also from Abraham's own family. Rivkah (Rebecca) was the granddaughter of his brother Nahor. Isaac brought her to his mother's tent and finally stopped grieving for the beloved Sarah. As with Sarah, Shabbat candles burned from one Friday to the next, and the challah was always fresh on the table. These aspects of the two mothers are meant to suggest not their preoccupation with domestic life but miracles associated with their holiness. The midrash associates the same characteristics with the Holy Temple in Jerusalem. There, a light always burned (the *ner tamid*, replicated in our synagogues today), and the shewbread was always fresh and warm. It is said also that Sarah's tent was always covered by a divine cloud, like the Mishkan or holy tabernacle in the desert.[8] The implication is that the holiness of Sarah's life was like that of the Temple itself, and that Rivkah echoed her in every detail.

But also like Sarah, Rivkah had a difficult passage to make: a struggle between two rivalrous sons over the family inheritance. For her, however, the issue was not clarified by the joy of a child's birth. After twenty (some say ten) years of childlessness, Rivkah found herself pregnant with twins. We know from the prophecy she received during her pregnancy that the crucial point of her destiny was in resolving their struggle; she was told that "two nations are in your womb" (Gen. 24:23). In their youth the two already flaunted their differences, and Jacob manipulated Esau into selling his birthright. Rivkah favored Jacob and saw more clearly than Isaac the weaknesses of Esau, the hunter, who was attached to material rather than spiritual things. The bond of the father with the firstborn was very strong, however, and Isaac loved Esau. Only Rivkah recognized that Jacob should alone carry on the spiritual inheritance from Abraham.

Rivkah found herself in the midst of an agonizing dilemma. To resolve it she acted dramatically—and in an apparently most unspiritual way: she helped Jacob disguise himself so that when his nearly blind father gave his deathbed blessings to the young men, he would give Jacob the blessing of the firstborn. Jacob at first objected to the idea, but Rivkah overruled him: "Let your curse be on me, my son; only listen to my voice, and go . . . " (Gen. 27:1). The ruse was a success, much to the dismay of Isaac and Esau. Esau was in a murderous rage. But Isaac accepted the situation and agreed with his wife to send Jacob away so that he would not be killed by his brother.

This act turned out to be the great work of Rivkah's life. She had found herself by God's providence the wife of a holy man: then, at a crucial juncture, she acted against him. She, who had been childless twenty years and had been devoted to her son (her case is the only one in which the Torah mentions that a woman "loved" a certain child, Gen. 25:28), now sent him away. Moreover, like Sarah, she had eagerly left the pagan atmosphere of her family to become Isaac's wife. Now she sent her son back to the land from which she had come. These decisions define the nature of motherhood as it is expressed in Rivkah.

What Rivkah teaches us seems first of all an extension of what we learn from the episodes of Sarah and Hagar. A woman is able to see the future by looking into the character of those around her—particularly, in these cases, the children. Sarah saw the character of Ishmael and had him banished from the household. Rivkah saw the character of Esau and contrived to have his father's favor taken away, then separated him from his brother by sending Jacob far away.

But we know that in the Torah, similar stories are not repeated merely to emphasize the same lesson again: Rivkah's story adds something new. The rivalrous sons were both her own sons, not children of two different wives; and she had to send her favorite son away, not, as in Sarah's case, the misbehaving one. In fact, Sarah's decision might be seen as promoting harmony and unity in the nuclear family. Rivkah's act perpetrated an opposite result: she had to divide the family and institute a separation whose length she did not know in order to preserve Jacob's life, protect him from ending up with Canaanite wives like his brother, and, she hoped, ensure the continuance of the family's spiritual heritage.

Such decisions sound extremely radical to us today. We learn very early in most modern families not to show favoritism toward one child. A mother of twins would be gently advised to treat the children equally while recognizing, in a positive way, their differences. Moreover, separation from a child at any age is extremely painful for a mother. Rivkah had to go on living in Canaan, dealing with Esau and her Canaanite daughters-in-law, while her beloved son was far away for some twenty years.

Most of us would probably have searched out any other route than this: send Jacob away for a few weeks or months, try to pacify Esau in the meantime, send for a wife from elsewhere—almost anything to keep the family together. It took not only courage, but a tremendous faith in her own inner knowledge, her own conviction that Jacob was the carrier of the family's spiritual heritage. Unity in the immediate family had to take second place to this.

Jacob certainly fulfilled her expectations: no sooner had he left his father's house than he experienced his famous dream of angels descending and ascending a ladder to heaven. His response was immediate: to establish a sanctuary to God in that place, henceforth known as Beth El. By this act he acknowledged his place in the lineage of spiritual fathers, and he maintained his separation from the surrounding paganism in all the years to come. He went on to marry two daughters of his mother's brother, thus fulfilling Rivkah's insights into his character and her hopes for his future.

In her own acts Rivkah belies the image of the matriarch as concerned merely with having children and being a helpmate to her husband. She was a woman of vision. However difficult her decisions, she was acting from her own inner sense of what was important in establishing the "house of Jacob" for the future. Moreover, it is clear from both the Torah text and the commentaries on these episodes that Rivkah's acts, like Sarah's, are considered every bit as important as the work of Abraham and Isaac. The men receive directions and promises from God; so do the women. Their concerns in following these out, however, are somewhat different. The men are engaged in the work of maintaining and settling their families and extended households, accumulating wealth, negotiating delicate territorial situations, defending their rights in a complex tribal society. The women focus on the inner workings of the family: how the relationships are developing, how each member of the family is being nourished, or abused, by others. From their point of view, this is the essence of providing for the future. The men settle matters in the external world, the women ensure the protection, nourishment, and challenge necessary to the spiritual health of the family. The explicit content of the spiritual heritage—God's promises regarding land and offspring—passes from father to son; the mother provides the environmment in which these can take root.

The greatness of the Mothers is not merely that they were prophets and visionaries. Beyond this, they understood that their passage through the seemingly ordinary events of pregnancy and birth was filled with significance for the future of their people and all of humanity. They knew that every decision they made had meaning—even if it might seem to others only a family matter. Without this, land, wealth, and ownership would have meant very little. Truth and the fulfillment of God's plan came from the treasure of holiness that they cherished in the inward, intimate sphere of their lives, just as much as from the work of Abraham and Isaac. This consciousness of inward treasure, preserved in the hands of women like Sarah and Rivkah was as important as, in later days, the Temple which preserved the treasure of the Jewish peoples' connection with God.

We can learn from Sarah and Rivkah about our own work today. In our families and communities, we make decisions every day about people in our care and in our sphere of influence—our children, our spouses, our elders, our coworkers, our neighbors. These shape the world just as surely as the decisions made in executive suites and at the political bargaining tables do. We assist or impede the spiritual growth of others with every word and act. As women of awareness, we manage the development of an inner treasure whose value far exceeds the material treasures of the nations of the earth. In that way, we follow Sarah's and Rivkah's example in every aspect of our lives.

Rachel and Leah, taken together, elaborate a different dimension of women's lives. Whereas the significant events and decisions portrayed in the Torah stories of Sarah and Rivkah focus on their concern for their family's destiny, Rachel and Leah are portrayed primarily as rivals in their relationship with their husband, Jacob. Here the "mother" must also face issues that come from being a wife and a woman among women.

Jacob favored Rachel from the beginning: he wanted to marry her first, but through a ruse his first wife turned out to be Leah instead. He who had fooled his brother was himself tricked by a disguise. Nevertheless, he did not indulge his frustration: he simply arranged with their father, Laban, to work for him an additional seven years in order to merit Rachel as well. They married, and Jacob continued to work to fill out his agreed term. But the conditions of the marriages clearly set the stage for an ongoing rivalry between the sisters.

The story line is simple: Leah knew that Rachel was Jacob's favorite, but she was fertile while Rachel was childless, so she hoped that by giving him many children she would win him to her. Rachel, frustrated in her situation, begged Jacob to pray for her that she would bear children. Like Channah much later, whose husband's other wife taunted her about her childlessness, being the favored wife did not satisfy her. Rachel gave Jacob her handmaid, who bore two children on her behalf. But Leah herself, meanwhile, gave Jacob six sons and a daughter, and two children by her handmaid. Rachel finally had two children of her own, Joseph and Benjamin, who became their father's favorites. She died in childbirth with the second.

Some facets of this story seem antiquated to us and distant: we are no longer part of a society where the number of children marks a woman's worth, and women are seldom taunted for inability to bear children. Not so strange to us, however, is rivalry between women, competition for the favors of a man on whatever basis, be it beauty, wealth, or charm. The anxiety demonstrated by both Rachel and Leah is familiar enough; their equal social status as Jacob's primary wives only exacerbated the conflict. Rachel had the upper hand but by no means felt secure in her position. The rivalry tore at each woman's sense of self-worth. It was an all-too-human situation. What is its spiritual significance?

Neither woman could accept her situation. Each knew (the midrash says the Mothers all knew prophetically) that she was one of four women who would bear children to Jacob; but this was not enough. Certainly, from the beginning of their marriages, they gave themselves over to that mission, but they did it in a way that made Jacob the ultimate judge of their success. The need to prove her worth in Jacob's eyes was fundamental to each woman. It might seem that Leah and Rachel were being seduced by the demands and values of patriarchal society. But, surprisingly, the biblical text takes a dim view of such values.

Jacob himself confronted Rachel directly on this issue. She asked him to pray for her, arguing—the midrash says—that, after all, his father, Isaac, had prayed for his Rivkah to be relieved of childlessness (see Gen. 25:21). He responded angrily: it is not I who am denying you children— God is the one who has closed your womb (Gen. 30:2). Jacob was turning her back to herself: if some flaw is causing this, you have to deal with God directly about it. Apparently this hit home. The Ramban (Nachmanides) tells us that Rachel devoted herself intensely to prayer, until her prayers were answered, as the Torah says: "And God listened to *her*" (Gen. 30:22).

Leah was anxious over her relationship with Jacob because he so clearly preferred Rachel. She hoped her bearing him sons would win his heart. She too judged herself by her success with Jacob. The story tells us how she named her first three sons, essentially as a reflection of her inner struggle over trying to capture Jacob's allegiance: "Reuven," because God looked on my affliction: (*ra-ah b'anyi*); "Shimon," because God heard I am hated (*snuah*); "Levi," because now my husband and I will be joined (*yilaveh*).

But something changed when the fourth was born. Rashi suggests that since Leah alone of Jacob's four wives had given him three children, she recognized she had already borne her share of the twelve he was destined to father. Her fourth was a special gift. In any case, she no longer named him out of her fragile sense of her relationship to Jacob, but turned outward: she called him "Yehudah," for "this time I will thank (or praise) the Lord" (*odeh*). The Talmud comments that "from the day the Holy One, Blessed be He, created His world, no man praised Him until Leah came and praised Him" (*Berachot* 7b). She truly opened her heart to God in thanksgiving. This was a significant movement for Leah, from seeing herself through Jacob's eyes to seeing herself as a woman of blessing.

This development in each of the women brings forth a problem that, according to modern psychology, haunts women today: defined so often by our relationships, we too readily depend on others for a sense of self-worth. We should not too readily identify this modern issue with the Torah story, however, for the Torah speaks not merely of a psychological problem, but of a spiritual one. We must look a little more closely at it.

The Genesis story of Adam and Chava gives us a clue: when God expelled them from the Garden after they ate the forbidden fruit, he declared that henceforth men would toil for sustenance, women would bear children in pain, and "her desire will be for her husband." One interpretation of this suggests it is part of woman's nature to seek approval from her husband and to identify herself through him.[8] This characteristic may not be a feature of patriarchal oppression but rather of the feminine psyche at the archetypal level: we often, perhaps unconsciously, choose to define ourselves in terms of our relationships to others, particularly to a husband, spiritually as well as psychologically.

Yet the Rachel and Leah stories suggest that a woman cannot always rest comfortably with a relationship to God established through her husband or children alone; in certain dimensions she must define it also for herself. Sarah and Rivkah clearly exemplify this: they sought and lis-

, not because
struggle and
man's weep-
one another
timately the
crifice that a
like our own
to heaven on

n with Jacob
's eyes were
from crying,
sights of this
rue: in deep
she came to
Rachel was
rael"—Jacob
wrestled on
ccompanied
e world, on
ther ances-
ther world,
and praise,
er than our

f the Torah
ve that can
a hero for
the years
into mar-
evotion to
Benjamin
st, repre-
outward
lovers, as
he whole
of God,

ensions
veloping

chel's prayer and Leah's praise of
oing development in this direction.
with God and through this came to
nt, either, that their development
, inward relation to God. For Jewish
nizes special feminine ability in the

a different dimension than the first
and inner knowledge seem to have
ers were a once whole entity that had
the resulting rivalry, disrupted their
often find that our fears, jealousies,
lt relationships instead of developing
upplication and Leah's thanksgiving
prayer, which for us too can lead us
r to God.
een the two sisters as two sides of life.
ith Jacob, each represented a different
nd soul. The sages describe this in a
ved in this life; Leah was his wife for
little more deeply.
Benjamin, Rachel was buried at Bet-
to bury her there, while they were
r body to the ancestral burying place in
a rather surprising decision. Certainly
tance to transport her, especially when
ph's coffins would later be brought all

achel was intended to be buried at Bet-
sents the exile of the Jewish people. She
ut to God on our behalf, asking him to
ophecy of Jeremiah, which we read on
ah, speaks of this tradition:

ah, and bitter weeping—Rachel weeping for
orted; they are no more. These are the words
ping, shed no more tears; there shall be a
n from the land of the enemy. You shall leave
shall return to their own land. (Jer. 31:15–17)

dlessness to an end, her tears will at last
odern woman's song by Shirah tells the

story: it is not by men's merit that God will bring us hon
of Abraham's tests or Isaac's devotion or Jacob's years
loneliness. God will bring us back to him because of a
ing.[9] Matters of the heart, of relationship, of our bonds
on this earth are the treasure of Rachel. She knew mos
bond to her husband and she knew in her death the
woman makes in bringing children into the world. Rachel
real mother: the one whose weeping and supplication ris
our behalf.

Of Leah, the rabbis say, her inner life and her true rela
are told in only three words: *V'einei Leah rakot*, "And Le
weak" (Gen. 29:17). While some say her eyes were sor
other commmentators explain that her eyes were not for th
world, but were attuned to a spiritual vision. Both could b
despair over her marital situation—out of her own weepin
a perception of God. Leah thus became Jacob's spiritual w
Jacob's favorite wife on one level, but Leah was the wife of
under his new name, given him by the angel with whom
the night before he crossed over into his homeland. Rache
him on his journey in the world, so she was buried out in
the road at Bet-lechem. Leah was buried with him and th
tors in the cave of Machpelah, for she was his wife for th
another level of being. Leah showed the path of thanksgivi
which comes, like the praise of the angels, from levels hi
ordinary life.

These descriptions of Rachel and Leah tell us somethir
perspective on married life. There are two dimensions to th
exist in marriage. The love of Jacob for Rachel was the lov
his princess: he served Laban for seven years to win her,
"seemed to him but a few days." Then, after Laban tricked
rying Leah instead, he served another seven years. Hi
Rachel continued in his relation to her sons: Joseph
remained dearest to him. The pair Israel and Leah, by c
sented a unity between man and woman that went beyon
appearances of ordinary married life. They were not rom
far as the world could see. But what is obvious is not alw
truth: there are hidden dimensions in marriage as in every
and these are revealed only with deeper understanding.

Correspondingly, Rachel and Leah actually stand for tw
of the Jewish people as a whole: Rachel for the changin

dimension of our action for good in this world, Leah for the eternal and unchanging soul-connection to God. Rabbi Nosson Scherman writes,

> Rachel represents Israel's role of dealing with the world, elevating it and ultimately conquering it. The actor playing this role changes according to his performance, and all of creation changes with him. This task is visible; moment by moment it challenges us. . . . Rachel was the sister who caught people's attention, she was the "beautiful" one who attracted the notice of people occupied with the activity of this world.
>
> . . . Leah is the quiet, unseen holiness of Israel. The Kabbalists refer to the world of Leah as the . . . *Hidden World.* Her world goes unnoticed in the hurly-burly of human activity, because it is holy and sublime beyond ordinary human comprehension. Her world is the soul of the universe as well as its ultimate goal, but it does not lower its standard to deal with the perceived "reality" of human activity. It is unseen. Scripture alludes to this when it speaks of Leah's eyes as being weak—figuratively, the "vision" needed to perceive the nature of Leah is too weak, too clouded by the tangible world that constantly occupies its attention.[10]

Rachel and Leah thus represent a twoness that is in all of us, and they hint at the rivalry, the conflict, that comes from our different allegiances to the world and to the eternal dimension of our souls.

Thus the Mothers of our tradition point to aspects of motherhood far beyond what we normally think of when we use the term *mother.* Their role was not merely to bear children, although often that aspect of life was pivotal for them in some way, as it is for many of us in our own lives. Equally significant is the way they symbolize various dimensions of our lives. They represent generativity, that dimension of creativity that looks toward the future. They not only tended and cared for what comes forth from them, they were also sensitive to the subtle nuances of life that made the difference between a truly spiritual development and a merely natural one, as in Isaac and Ishmael, Jacob and Esau.

The Mothers also represent inner strength and power. They were willing to use their influence and power to direct the inner life of the family according to their best—in their cases prophetic—insight. They made sharp and difficult decisions, even when it meant facing a conflict or a separation from husband or children. Their inner knowledge gave them that strength.

The stories of the Mothers show women struggling for, and developing, their own sense of self-worth by turning to God. Joyful faith and a sense of gratitude and blessing emerge, in different ways, from these stories. Sarah brings laughter into our religious life, in a this-worldly affirmation of faith, surprise, and joy. Rivkah shows us an awesome strength and certainty and, like Sarah, a commanding voice. Leah brings comfort; from her we know that the quality of the life beyond is available now, as we offer thanks and praise to God who provides all we need. Rachel, with her death in childbirth, preserves for us the undying faith that our deepest hopes for the world will be realized. From her we know that all our weeping for our children, for our loved ones, for life itself will not be in vain: we will yet come home, there will yet be peace. From all our Mothers we have the gift of a deeply feminine reality, lived with strength and passion, the grounding of our past and the direction of our future.

CHAPTER 2

Womanhood and Sexuality

An important aspect of our search for appropriate feminine models is the issue of sexuality. While nearly everyone recognizes that Judaism has a fundamentally positive attitude toward sexuality (in contrast to more ascetic traditions), it has also been claimed that Judaism regards female sexuality as dangerous and, for this reason, has confined women to a limited sphere of action. There are some grounds for this claim: the traditional separation of men and women in public prayer is largely based on concern about the distractions and lustful thoughts that might arise if men and women prayed in a mixed group.[1] The *Pirke Avot*, one of the favored ethical texts of classical Judaism, warns that one should not converse with a woman,[2] and this is buttressed in the aggadic tradition by stories of righteous men being overthrown by the seductive powers of women. Further, while halacha requires both men and women to dress modestly, women receive far more instruction and exhortation concerning this requirement.

Feminists have objected to the attitudes toward women embedded in these examples, arguing that they represent a misogynist view, seeing women as sex objects and men as helpless victims. Even if it is true that female sexuality is more provocative to men than the reverse, women should not have to be responsible for men's inability to control their lusts. Perhaps, some have suggested (usually jokingly), men should be socially confined instead of women. At least, restrictions should be equally imposed and observed by both sexes.

There is, however, another curious twist to this discussion. While women in some ways are regarded as more sexual, and dangerously so, they are also regarded in Jewish tradition as more spiritual. Many rabbis hold that women are obligated in fewer mitzvot because they do not need to perform certain commandments (for example, the external appurtenances of *tallit* and *tefillin*) to achieve a high level of spirituality. Other major religious traditions, more influenced by asceticism, have held that the sexuality of woman implied her spiritual inferiority—for example, the idea in some forms of Buddhism that a woman must be reborn as a man in order to reach enlightenment. Such attitudes were so deeply enmeshed in Christianity that, in the early middle ages, monks debated whether women had souls. In Judaism, however, the two qualities of intense sexuality and intense spirituality are not mutually exclusive.

This paradox suggests that this argument is not a simple one about how women should dress or whether men and women should be separated in the synagogue. Underlying these issues is a fundamental debate about the sexual nature of women, its power in human society, and its relation to spirituality. A full understanding of this matter would, I believe, lead to a resolution of many social issues that revolve around gender. But that is beyond the scope of the current discussion. We simply wish to come to a better understanding of the traditional Jewish perspective on these matters, and we can do this by looking closely at a few more of the feminine models we have in Jewish tradition.

Several of our great heroines were known for their personal attractiveness, including their physical beauty and, in some cases, their seductive qualities. This means that while Jewish women are warned about their sexual power, and men are warned to be watchful of it, many of our models of righteousness are attractive women who in fact use their sexuality to accomplish certain purposes. These women are also, of course, regarded as paragons of piety. We will look briefly at four: Ruth, who stepped past the normal bounds of modesty to establish herself in a new household; Tamar, who bypassed the given marriage rules to entice her father-in-law, Judah; Esther, who gave herself to the harem of a non-Jewish king; and Yehudit, who seduced the general of an opposing army and slew him mercilessly. All these women are examples of virtue in the service of Jewish ideals. In what follows, we will see what we can learn from them about our own nature and purpose as sexual beings in the world.

Great ancestresses,
Great grandmothers of King David himself
Lovely women,
Ruth and Tamar.
A surprise to see such women,
Choosing,
Determining,
Risking.
Is this the power of the Way
That will lead ultimately
To redemption?

We often hold in our minds the stereotype of the woman of ancient times—whether in China, India, or the Middle East—as submissively being bought and sold, in slavery or in marriage. Certainly, marriages arranged by the parents, formalized by negotiations between the fathers, were the rule in many societies, and Jewish communities were not an exception. It should be noted, of course, that these marriages did not necessarily give the young man any more freedom of choice than the woman; and, in rabbinic Judaism at least, a woman was not to be married to a man without her consent.[3] Nonetheless, it cannot be denied that arranged marriages appear to us an extreme restriction on a woman's freedom of choice. It is well worth noting, therefore, that Jewish tradition celebrates two famous women who found themselves in situations where the standard procedure of marriage simply had not worked out for them. As a result, they decided to take matters into their own hands and in bold ways rearranged their lives within a fundamentally patriarchal marriage system.

The first story is that of Ruth, the account of whose life we read at the holiday of Shavuot. Ruth was a Moabite princess who had been married to a Jewish man—he had come to Moab with his father, mother, and brother during a famine in Israel. His brother also had married a Moabite. But the father and two sons died, leaving the mother, Naomi, alone with her two daughters-in-law. Naomi decided to return to her kin in Israel and urged her daughters-in-law to return to their father's homes. One did. But Ruth, who had come to love Jewish ways, begged Naomi to take her back to Israel too. "Where you go, I will go, and where you stay,

I will stay. Your people shall be my people, and your God my God" (Ruth 1:16–17). Thus Ruth became the most famous of converts to Judaism.

Back in Israel, however, Naomi and Ruth were not in the best of positions. Naomi's husband had lost his fortune in Moab, and she was nearly penniless except for some family land. Ruth took the responsibility upon herself to provide for them both by following the gleaners in the field, collecting sheaves of grain from what they dropped, as was the custom among the poor. While gathering, she was noticed by Boaz, a well-to-do kinsman of Naomi and himself a widower, who treated Ruth kindly and encouraged his workers to drop extra grain for her.

When Ruth told Naomi of Boaz's kindness to her, Naomi advised her to take the initiative: to go at night to the threshing floor, where Boaz slept during the harvest season, and let him know of her interest in him.

She came in quietly, turned back the covering at his feet, and lay down. About midnight something disturbed the man as he slept; he turned over and, behold, there was a woman lying at his feet. "Who are you?" he asked. "I am your servant, Ruth," she replied. "Now spread your skirt over your servant, because you are my next-of-kin." (Ruth 3:7–9)

Boaz, who was elderly, praised her for her loyalty in looking for a husband from among the family: "You haven't gone searching out some young man, rich or poor." But he did not accept her offer immediately, because, he said, there was a closer relative than he who had the right to take Ruth as a wife. She slept there, however, and the next day Boaz met with the other man and made the legal arrangements to claim Ruth as his wife. Not only Ruth but also Naomi was thereby provided for. Soon after, Ruth bore a son, Oved, who was the grandfather of King David.

Tradition praises Ruth greatly for her modesty in dress and demeanor; indeed, the midrash says this was one of the great virtues Boaz saw in her. Yet, on Naomi's advice, she dared to attract Boaz's attention by a route quite outside the ordinary rules of modesty. Rather than Naomi inquiring among the relatives or finding a male relative to speak on Ruth's behalf, the women took direct action. None of this was public, of course—no one but Boaz and Naomi knew that Ruth had come to the threshing-room floor. But it was a forthright act from a woman otherwise exemplary for her modesty and retiring nature.

At the same time, we should remember that it was this same Ruth who had left the familiar comforts of her Moabite home—where, tradition has it, she was of noble family—to live in a new society where she would be treated for some time as a stranger. She had already made one bold move, following the righteous and kind Naomi in order to better her life morally and spiritually. In a sense she had taken the older woman as her spiritual guide: "Where you die, I will die; and there I will be buried." Then, with Boaz, she was willing to take a still greater step—exposing herself to the risk of public shame—to secure a husband who exemplified the kindness she had admired in Naomi and to make a place for herself in the new society. In short, Ruth put her womanhood and reputation on the line in order to shape her own future.

A similar kind of daring marks the personality of Tamar. Her story appears, almost as a diversion, in the middle of the familiar and engrossing stories of Joseph and his brothers in the book of Genesis. While most Hebrew school children can tell us the Joseph stories in great detail, we are unlikely to hear the tale of Tamar and Judah (Yehudah)—the sexual motif is rather too explicit for younger pupils.

Judah, a son of Jacob by Leah, had three sons by a Canaanite woman. When his firstborn son, Er, was old enough, Judah arranged for him to marry Tamar, who according to rabbinic tradition was the daughter of a *cohen* (priest). Unfortunately, Er died almost immediately. According to the law of levirate marriage, the second son, Onah, would fulfill his duty by marrying Tamar and fathering a child in his brother's name. Onah married her, but apparently not willingly; for he committed the sin of "spilling his seed," thus making it impossible for her to bear a child for Er. For this God brought death to Onah as well. Tamar, as a result, found herself engaged to the third son of Judah, Shelah, who was yet too young to marry. Judah sent Tamar back to live in her father's house until the wedding could be performed.

Time passed, and Judah did not call her back to the marriage canopy, so Tamar took things into her own hands. When she heard that Judah would be passing through her neighborhood on the way to a sheepshearing, she disguised herself as a prostitute and sat at a crossroads. When Judah traveled by, she enticed him to come in. He offered her payment in the form of one of his sheep, and she agreed, but with the proviso that until he paid her he should leave with her his cloak, staff, and ring. He did as she asked. But when a servant returned with the sheep, he could find no prostitute nor anyone that knew her. Judah, of course, had no idea as to her real identity.

A few months passed, and Judah was informed that his daughter-in-law, who was supposed to be living chastely in her father's home waiting to marry Shelah, was pregnant. Furious at the shame she thus brought to his household, he demanded that she be brought to him so that she could be punished as befitted her crime and her status as a priest's daughter: death by fire. Tamar came when sent for; but she sent ahead to Judah the items he had left with her, along with the message: "The man to whom these belong is the father of my child." Judah immediately recognized the items and remembered the unknown harlot. "She is more righteous than I," he proclaimed, "because I did not marry her to my son" (Gen. 38:25–26). Henceforth she was a full member of the family, as his own wife. From the union between Judah and Tamar, twins were born, Perez and Zerach. Perez was to be an ancestor of Boaz (Ruth's husband) and therefore also of King David.

Like Ruth, Tamar took a considerable risk, not only with her reputation, but also with her life. Had Judah recognized her through her disguise, he could have had her killed for playing the prostitute. Or even after she had sent him the personal items identifying him as the father of the child, he could have pretended ignorance and let her die. As it happened—and probably as Tamar expected—Judah was also a righteous man and would not let a child he had fathered go unacknowledged. Nevertheless, her ploy to get pregnant by Judah himself, after so much trouble had passed between her and his sons, was a daring move in and of itself.

We can imagine that Tamar had other alternatives. She appears to have been from a significant family; eventually she, or her father, could have used legal means to force Judah to marry her to Shelah. Perhaps she feared Judah would have resisted her direct attempts to gain her marital rights. Judah may have regarded her as a woman bewitched—after all, two of his sons had died after marrying her. Thus, like Ruth, she bypassed what would appear to have been the more normal legal and social routes. In a sense she played the part he gave her: a woman of strange and dangerous sexual powers, she took on the disguise of a harlot. To attract Judah, she must have been, as we would say, bewitchingly beautiful and sexually attractive.

Tamar was a woman not to be satisfied with halfway measures, unfulfilled promises, or compromises. Her plans for marriage and family frustrated, she went directly to the source of the problem, Judah himself. She stepped out of her garb of mourning for her dead husbands and into the realm of her personal power through her sexuality. Then she returned calmly to her father's household, awaiting the turn of events she knew would come. And, the story attests, her strategy was a righteous one. The midrash comments that she knew she was destined to have a child from the family of Judah, destined to be an ancestress of King David. Instead of waiting for Shelah, however, she became Judah's own partner.

What is perhaps most remarkable is not that there existed women who in unusual cases bypassed the normal social system or normal course of law to accomplish their ends—to solidify their position, as with Ruth, or to restore justice, as with Tamar. More surprising, in view of the strong legal framework of Judaism and the supposedly patriarchal attitudes of the tradition, is that such women's lives would be praised. What is it about them that deserved such praise, even though in other contexts their actions might be criticized?

Clearly it is not the acts themselves that made Ruth and Tamar righteous women but their total orientation in life. They appear at first glance to have acted out of self-interest. But the traditions about them affirm quite the opposite. Boaz praised Ruth for her loyalty. That aspect of her character was so strong that she could do something that, while within the law, would have been frowned on if generally known. But her strong sense of connection to the Jewish people, and to Naomi in particular, enabled her to see the right way to reconstruct the family that had been broken with the departure of Naomi's family from Israel and the subsequent deaths of her husband and sons. Similarly, Tamar was extolled for her righteousness: she saw justice being undone and saw how it could be restored. She understood the law and its spirit. Rather than embarrass Judah before a court of justice, she found a woman's way and, trusting in his righteousness as well, fulfilled the law's intent.

In both stories women's extraordinary acts do not undo morality but restore it. First of all, they acted, like the Mothers in chapter 1, from deep inner knowledge. Ruth, Naomi, and Tamar were able to see connections and implications that had escaped the other people involved; they went on to act directly to restore the balance. More than that, the fact that the stories put their boldness in a sexual framework is not meant to legitimize sexual freedom. Rather, it tells us about the depth of their actions: they were acting from their essential being as women. Mind, heart, and body united to restore the balance of righteousness. This, the stories tell us, is a special dimension of women's action. Sexuality may have its dangers, but it can also be transformed by righteous action to serve the highest purpose—indeed, to pave the way for the Messiah and the age of perfection, just as Tamar's and Ruth's descendants gave birth to King David.

Esther, dream of our childhood,
As girls in pink satin and lace
we wore your crown
and curtsied with you before the king
and denounced the villain!
Your sisters now,
we peek behind the veils of your private chambers—
What secrets lie there for us?

Queen Esther lives in the memories of most of us as a kind of Jewish fairy-tale figure—a flawlessly beautiful heroine whom everyone loved and admired, who conquered the forces of evil and saved the kingdom. Nearly every young girl dressed up like Queen Esther for at least a few Purim celebrations and coveted the Esther role in the Purim play. But is Esther more than a girlish dream? Is there a modern meaning for us in her story?

Let us briefly review the events recounted in Megillas Esther—the biblical book of Esther. Sometime in the late sixth or fifth century B.C.E. (exact dates are debated[4]) the Jewish community of Persia found itself under threat of extermination from some elements in their host country, owing to the powerful anti-Semitic influence of a villain known in Jewish tradition as Haman. Haman was prime minister to a king entitled Ahashverus (perhaps one of the Persian kings known otherwise as Cyrus, Xerxes, or Artaxerxes). The account of a Queen Esther, or of Haman's specific plot, is not found elsewhere, but the events could have occurred in the reign of Cyrus or in the following century.

The unfolding was as follows: Ahashverus's consort was at first Queen Vashti, but after she refused to entertain his friends by appearing nude at one of his banquets, he had her executed. He soon decided to select a new queen from among the most beautiful women of the land, and his choice fell on a Jewish woman, Esther. Esther was the niece—some say the wife, or both—of a well-known Jew named Mordecai. He allowed her to join Ahashverus's harem and be crowned queen and advised her to keep her Jewish identity secret. The midrash tells how she went to great lengths to keep Jewish customs, particularly Shabbat and the dietary laws, while keeping her Jewishness a secret.

As Haman rose to power, he was particularly offended by Mordecai, who refused to bow to Haman as a rightful representative of the king. In his rage Haman devised a plot against all the Jews, persuading Ahashverus to issue a decree that all other citizens of the realm should attack the Jews as traitors. Mordecai led the Jewish community in fasting and prayer and asked Esther to intervene with the king. At first she hesitated in fear of her life—for it was forbidden to approach the Persian despot without some initiative from him—but finally agreed.

Esther invited the king and his chief minister, Haman, to a private banquet, flattering them both with much attention. Then at a second banquet she revealed her Jewish identity and exposed Haman's plot. In some of the delightful twists of the story, Haman ended up having to lead Mordecai through the streets as a hero mounted on a royal horse—a role he thought would be his—and was later hanged on the very gallows he had prepared for Mordecai. Ultimately, the decree against the Jews was superseded by a second decree allowing them to fight back against any attackers; the Jews of Persia emerged victorious, and Mordecai ended up as one of the king's principal advisers.

The ins and outs of the story have made it popular material for annual plays, with Mordecai and Esther, of course, the favorite characters among the children. The theme of fighting anti-semitism in the communities of exile have kept it relevant among adults for more than two thousand years. Esther has continued to be discussed and taught, particularly among women, as Purim approaches every year; among adult women as well as girls, she is regarded as one of the greatest of Jewish heroines.

Yet some recent feminist interpreters, reacting perhaps against the fairy-tale perfection of the Jewish queen, have objected to this idealization of Esther. Instead, they have tried to resurrect Vashti as the real heroine of the Megillah. After all, they argue, Vashti stood up bravely to Ahashverus, refusing to appear naked as entertainment for his men's party. (This ignores the midrashic commentary that tells us it was Vashti's vanity that made her so brave—she did not want them to see the marks of disease that were on her skin!) Esther, in this view, remained demure and retiring, a compliant member of the harem, until the eleventh hour; and even then she was largely following Mordecai's instructions.[5]

Pointing at Vashti highlights what is perhaps the main concern of feminist writers in approaching issues of sexuality: a woman's first priority is to fight all attempts to make her a sex object. The objectification of women, discussed at length by modern feminist writers from Simone de Beauvoir onward, looms large in any modern attempt to rectify malefemale relations. We should understand, however, that this was simply not an issue for Jewish writers in earlier times. This was not because women accepted that they were sex objects. On the contrary, women were viewed as complex beings with many significant qualities, and a powerful sexual presence was one of those qualities. They regarded themselves, and were regarded, as very different from men. The ability to bear and mother children was one of those differences, the quality of their sexuality was another. The objectification of that sexuality—making it a commodity to be separated, bought, and sold on a large scale—is largely the product of modern society and particularly of the pornographic industry. Women, indeed, were bought and sold in earlier times (as were men and children), but many factors went into those exchanges, not necessarily only the desire of a man for more sex objects to gratify his desires.

Yet sexuality, attractiveness, seductiveness were part of the personality of a woman who was desired by men and admired (or envied) by other women. We have seen in the stories of Sarah that she was regarded as so attractive that she was whisked off to Pharaoh's household immediately on arriving in Egypt; the Canaanite prince Avimelech also found her nearly irresistible. Esther is presented much the same way (indeed, Rashi finds a hint of their similarity in numerology: Sarah lived 127 years, and Esther ruled 127 provinces).

Both found themselves, because of their beauty, in the palaces of foreign kings. This frank acknowledgment of women's sexual powers and charm is an aspect of women's being that feminists prefer to ignore. It seems a barrier to full participation in society. But this puts us in the unfavorable position of denying the obvious—namely, that women in general and in different degrees have enormous power to arouse sexual feelings in men. These feelings can be strong, even overwhelming or uncontrollable. It is pointless, and ultimately destructive to women themselves, to deny this power. What we must do is retrieve it from the grasp of pornographic culture and rediscover its place in our own lives.

In this respect the story of Esther can enlighten us. Esther may seem a bit too compliant for modern-day tastes. But the other side of the coin is that once having been chosen among all the beauties of Persia as the king's favorite, she recognized that her beauty was in this situation her trump card. It would not have been her best move, when Haman began to stir up anti-semitic feelings, to organize protest marches around the palace. Her personal power over the king was what counted—and, with this king, that meant her beauty and sexual attractiveness. Boaz might appreciate loyalty, but Ahashverus cared only about the sensual realm. At first Esther did not know how her personal assets would eventually bring her to a heroic opportunity—risking her life in an attempt to foil

Haman's plot. But she, and Mordecai, knew or sensed where her power lay, and she protected it even to the point of hiding her Jewish identity.

Esther, then, gives us a clue as to the role of female sexuality in establishing our own identity. Sexual power is part of a woman's inherent power—differing in degree, quality, and extent for each woman. But it cannot remain a viable source of power when squandered: it must be guarded and used in its own proper time. Perhaps, indeed, Vashti sensed this when she refused to grant the king's most outrageous request, but for her it was too late. As a willing partner in his flamboyant hedonism up until then—she too was known for her lavish parties—she had lost her effectiveness in this realm. Esther followed a different path, to the good of the Jews of Persia.

This sense of hidden power is, I think, important to our understanding of the feminine. Lynn Gottlieb has observed that Esther was a special heroine to Marrano women because they perceived themselves, like Esther, as living a secret existence different from the reality perceived by the outside world.[6] Kim Chernin's recent novel *The Flame Bearers* explores the theme of a hidden women's tradition within Judaism. Legends often tell of the "mysteriousness" of women, of our "secret" lore. These are not merely reactions to patriarchy: out of fear or self-protection we hide our real selves. Rather, we know deeply that some forms of power are best kept secret, guarded from public scrutiny, and used with great care. Esther's name is sometimes interpreted as meaning "hidden," as in *hester punim*—the "hidden face" of God; and God's name is never mentioned in the Megillah—the divine is hidden too. This is one of the deep dimensions of women's lives.

Yehudit,
strange soldier of war!
Bearing gifts
to delight the senses,
cheeses and wines,
soft temptation.
You will make his bed
and let him die on it.
Lighting the Chanukkah candles,
we renew ourselves,
remembering you.

The book of Judith, in Hebrew *Yehudit*, is one of the least known of our tradition, being part of the Apocrypha to the Bible. Yet it is one of the books to accompany a holiday: like the Song of Songs for Pesach, Ruth for Shavuot, and Esther for Purim, the book of Yehudit is read during Chanukkah. Its violent events and its relatively lesser known historical context may account for its fading into the background. For women, all the more: I have found that many women do not relish the story of Yehudit. But its impact on me was powerful when I first began to examine female models and the issue of sexuality. Yehudit represents sexuality in the service of the Jewish people, in truly a life-or-death context, as no other Jewish heroine does.

Since the story is less well known than Esther's, it is worth recounting at some length. The book was probably set down in its present form during the Maccabean period—certainly it reflects the Maccabees' passion for heroic defense of the land and the Temple. It re-creates, however, events long past. In the late sixth or early fifth century B.C.E., not long after Jews had returned from exile in Babylon and rebuilt the Temple, the threat of destruction again appeared from the north. Another "Nebuchadnezzar" had arisen and conquered the Medes; he vowed now to subjugate those nations who had not obeyed his request to assist him in that war. Most of the peoples from Damascus to Samaria bowed to his huge army, led by the indomitable general Holofernes. Holofernes destroyed temples and altars throughout those lands and demanded that the people worship his "god," Nebuchadnezzar the king. The Jews of Judea, however, chose to resist, lest they lose their beloved Temple which they had so recently restored.

The Jews fortified themselves on the hilltop towns guarding the approach to Jerusalem. Holofernes, who had been warned that the Jews could not be defeated unless they sinned against their God, followed a cautious approach, setting siege to the town of Bethulia. For more than a month he controlled the water supplies. Exhausted, the town's magistrates declared that they could last only five more days; if God did not deliver them, they would surrender.

Into this situation stepped Yehudit, a widow of three years who was extremely pious—she still dressed in mourning clothes, fasted a great deal, and devoted herself to prayer. She excoriated the magistrates for daring to put deadlines on God, then formed her own plan to undermine the opposing army. The book offers us her remarkable prayer, where she begged that the God who avenged Dinah—Leah and Jacob's daughter who had been raped by Shechem—should grant her success. Note the implicit comparison of the "pollution" of Dinah's womb to the feared pollution of the Holy Temple by the Assyrians:

O Lord, God of my forefather Shimon! You put in his hand a sword to take venge-ance on those foreigners who had stripped off a virgin's veil to defile her, uncov-ered her thighs to shame her, and polluted her womb to dishonor her. You said, "It shall not be done," yet they did it. So you gave up their rulers to be slain, and their bed, which blushed for their treachery, to be stained with blood. . . . You gave up their wives as booty, and their daughters as captives, and all their spoils to be divided among your beloved sons who, aflame with zeal for your cause and aghast at the pollution of their blood, called on you to help. O God, you are my God, hear now a widow's prayer. . . .

You see the Assyrians assembled in their strength, proud of their horses and riders, boasting of the power of their infantry, and putting their faith in shield and javelin, bow and sling. They do not know that you are the Lord who stamps out wars; the Lord is your name. Shatter their strength by your power and crush their might in your anger. For they have planned to desecrate your sanctuary, to pollute the dwelling-place of your glorious name, and to strike down the horns of your altar with the sword. Mark their arrogance, pour your wrath on their heads, and give to me, widow as I am, the strength to achieve my end. Use the deceit on my lips to strike them dead . . . shatter their pride by a woman's hand. For your might lies not in numbers nor your sovereign power in strong men; but you are the God of the humble, the help of the poor, the support of the weak, the protec-tor of the desperate, the deliver of the hopeless. (Yehudit 9:2–11)

Yehudit crossed enemy lines to offer herself as an adviser to Holofernes. She led him to believe that the defenders of Bethulia could soon be defeated, because they had decided to violate the Jewish dietary laws in their desperate fight against death from the siege. If he would only wait a few days until they had received permission from the sages in Jerusalem to eat the forbidden food, they would be at his mercy. By this explanation she persuaded him to accept her as an ally and at the same time to allow her to continue practicing her religion—she claimed to have left her people because they were traitors to her faith while she herself remained dedicated. While Holofernes waited, however, he decided he would entertain this woman, lest others laugh at him for letting such an opportunity pass by. She accepted his invitation to his tent and engaged him entertainingly, plying him with wine and cheeses. In his excitement he ate and drank too much, and when he fell asleep, Yehudit took his own sword and beheaded him with it.

Yehudit had already made it a practice, with permission from Holofer-nes, to go out of the camp before dawn every morning to pray. With this pretext, she was able to leave in the early morning hours, carrying the head wrapped in Holofernes' bed canopy, and take it to the Jewish camp. The next morning it was displayed before the Assyrian army. When the soldiers realized their general had been killed, their morale was broken and the Jewish army routed them easily.[7] Yehudit became the heroine of the age: she lived to the age of 105, never remarried, and was buried with her husband in his tomb. And, the book concludes, no one dared to rise up against Israel again during her lifetime or for long after.

Few Jewish heroines achieved the public stature accorded to Yehudit. Yet, admired and acclaimed by all—her fame continued to increase throughout her lifetime, it is said—she refused to use her influence to gain power. She could probably have married into a powerful family, but she chose to remain unmarried, to continue living on her husband's estate, and to divide her property among his close relatives when she died. We may assume that she made devotion to the God of Israel and the Jewish laws her primary focus, just as she had during the campaign against Holofernes.

As in the case of Esther, Yehudit appears to us as a woman who guarded her power, remaining modest and somewhat retiring despite her fame. Before the episode with Holofernes, she had been living as a pious mourner far longer than the law required; but when the moment came, her full womanly power emerged to be used for the good. It is clearer in her story than in Esther's, moreover, that she saw her power, including her sexual power, as directly derived from her spirituality: she appealed to God as a "poor widow," a devout mourner, that he would turn the "deceit of her lips" into a strength for good. She transformed herself literally overnight from an apparently passive, inwardly focused woman into a seductress, revealing before the Assyrian general and his host the beauty, passion, and intelligence that had lain hidden beneath her mourning clothes. "Who can despise a nation," exclaimed Holofernes' soldiers, "which has such women as this! We must not leave one alive, for if they escape they will outwit the whole world!" (Ydt. 10:19)

Yehudit revealed herself as capable of even more than they imagined: killing their leader. This was no simple task, and it involved a great deal of risk to herself. Her strategy was many-layered: a story to deceive Holofernes about her people and herself, a time of patient waiting that required a great deal of composure, a plot to get him drunk, and courage to kill the enemy. She had to use her intelligence, her self-control, her beauty and sexual attractiveness, and her physical strength. The culmination in a seduction is somewhat disturbing to modern sensibilities. But the story is not a moral lesson in a direct sense; it is not advising women to use sex to exploit a man's vulnerability in order to do him in. Rather, the point is archetypal, about the essential being of women. We have a strong sexual dimension, and when we act as total beings, our sexuality, our physical being, is an integral part of that action.

This comes out clearly, I think, in the remarkable vision of womanhood revealed in Yehudit's prayer. In her passionate appeal she addressed God as the God of Shimon, Jacob's son—rather than more traditionally as the God of Abraham, Isaac, and Jacob—for Shimon was the one who led the Israelite men in vengeance on behalf of Dinah. Yehudit did not call for vengeance for spilled blood, however, since the Assyrians had as yet killed no Judeans. Rather, she begged God to protect the sanctuary in Jerusalem from pollution and defilement, just as Shimon avenged the defilement of his sister. For Yehudit the Holy Temple was holy as a woman's body is holy, and her God was the guardian of this kind of holiness against all those who would defile it.[8]

Yehudit brings together for us the connection of sexuality with spirituality. We saw earlier that Ruth and Tamar were willing to take personal risks, Ruth with reputation and Tamar with her life, by offering themselves to a man for the sake of a righteous outcome. With Esther we saw that she could guard her sexual attractiveness, then use it to influence King Ahashverus and save the Jewish people; Yehudit did the same with Holofernes. All these women were acting out of a deep conviction, a profound spiritual consciousness that their acts were righteous.

Yet Yehudit more than the others brings out the inner connection of action and purpose. Sexuality was not simply a tool to achieve some worldly purpose—whether to capture a man's love or to win a battle. For Yehudit, the means was intimately connected to the end. The danger of polluting the Temple was like the threat of rape: to prevent that horrific act, Yehudit could take the risk of offering herself to Holofernes. Fortunately her plot succeeded, and she did not have to submit to him. But the viewpoint of the story is that when a woman offers herself, it is an act of holiness, like an offering in the Temple. We have already seen the connection of woman and Temple in the allusion to Sarah and Rivkah's tents (p. 11). Now Yehudit deepens the connection in her view of sexuality. When a woman acts in sexual way, she must regard herself as holy. The end she wishes to achieve must be holy as well—not just to get married, but to fulfill a special destiny; not just to wield power, but to save the Jewish people. It follows that Yehudit, Esther, Ruth, and Tamar had to be otherwise chaste, modest, and pious. And the reverse images, of the harlot or the adulterous woman, are such powerfully negative ones in Israelite literature precisely because the image of sexual holiness is so strong.

The stories tell us not merely that women are sensual and can use that power to men's detriment. That would be a manipulative use of sex, certainly not to be admired. Rather, they tell us sexuality is holy, to be used only in the service of holiness; and women have direct access to that holy power. From this deep view of women's bodies comes the high Jewish valuation of marriage and sex only within marriage. From it also comes the knowledge that when women do not value this aspect of themselves, they dilute their power. Sex becomes at best mere pleasure, at worst manipulative and dishonest. And this does not merely mean dishonest to our feelings; many modern advisers would have it that sex is all right if we are personally honest about it. The feminine models in Judaism tell us that sex used any other way than for holiness is dishonest to God, dishonest to the purpose of our feminine being. The woman who knows her sexuality and her inner, spiritual self can recognize her true purpose in life, can act with power and confidence at any moment, and can thereby affect her own destiny, the destiny of her people, and that of the whole world.

CHAPTER 3

Commanding Voices

History
weighs on us sometimes—
some say it is his-story only!
Where have all the women gone?
Gone to sweep floors and gather dust?
Or gone to other worlds,
Gone to save us, every one?

It is only natural to ask, if women are such a strong presence in Jewish life and lore, why is it that we have heard of so few, in comparison, say, to the long lists of kings or rabbis that we find in our history books? We know of women who were scholars and models of piety: Beruria, who was considered the equal of any man in the early talmudic period, Rashi's daughters in early medieval times. Yet they seem to be exceptions.

An answer that goes beyond the superficial requires some investigation and analysis, so we must depart from looking at individual figures. But first, two more stories to which we will return at the end of this chapter.

In the first century B.C.E.—less than a century after the victory of the Maccabees over the Hellenistic Syrian governors—the land of Israel found itself once more embroiled in internal and external disputes. Many of the Jewish leaders of the period, in contrast to their Maccabean ancestors, sought alliances with powerful Hellenistic rulers. Internally, the ruling Hasmonean dynasty had become intertwined with the priesthood ever since Simon, the last of the Maccabee brothers, had been proclaimed both high priest and king of an independent Judea (142 B.C.E.), thus centralizing power to an extreme. In this situation political machinations and treachery in the courts were rampant.

Under Simon's son Johanan Hyrcanus, the land under Jewish rule had been greatly expanded. On his death (104 B.C.E.), he granted the secular rulership to his wife and the high priesthood to his son Judah Aristobulus. Aristobulus promptly imprisoned his mother; one tradition has it that he had her starved to death. He put three of his four brothers in jail as well and killed the fourth when he suspected him of treachery. His wife, Shulamit Alexandra, stayed safely in the background. Fortunately, this tyrant reigned only one year.

Queen Shulamit released the brothers and married the eldest, Alexander Jannai, in accordance with the law of levirate marriage. Alexander was involved in war for almost his entire reign of twenty-seven years (103–76 B.C.E.). At first he was favored by the popular religious party, the Pharisees (precursors of the rabbinic tradition). But when they requested that he give up the high priesthood and keep only the kingship, he was enraged. For most of his reign he favored the more aristocratic Sadducees. Sometimes his acts against the Pharisees were quite violent. Once when he appeared in the high priests's garb on Sukkot at the ceremony of water libation, the people pelted him with their *etrogim* (the citron fruit used in the holiday ritual). In retribution he sent his mercenary army against them, killing six thousand followers of the Pharisees. Shulamit, however, continued to maintain her religious principles and, despite her husband's hatred of them, stayed in close relationship with the party of the Pharisees.

At the same time, Shulamit had gained the love and admiration of the people of Israel. Toward the end of his reign, Alexander decided to leave things in her hands, for he saw, as the historian Josephus said, that the people would bow to her authority as to no other. He also softened his attitude toward the Pharisees and advised Shulamit to make peace with the parties. On his death she became sole ruler, at the age of sixty-three.

Her reign, though only ten years in length, became known as the "golden age" of the Hasmoneans. Remarkably, she managed to maintain internal peace, and external enemies were quiet during this time as well. She distributed power by giving her younger son, Aristobulus, charge of the army, and the high priesthood to the elder, Hyrcanus. She surrounded herself with advisers from among the Pharisees and reorganized the high state council so that many more individuals, mostly Pharisees, participated in the government. But she was not punitive toward the Sadducees, the leading competing party. She doubled the size of the army by recruitment rather than by hiring mercenaries, thus making the army more an arm of the people. Through extensive treaties she kept the country out of damaging wars, allowing only one expedition by her son Aristobulus. The relief the nation experienced, after having been torn by wars for years, was enormous.

Thus, although Shulamit had remained in the background for twenty-eight years, she emerged as a powerful figure able to balance the demands of an extraordinarily difficult political situation and stabilize her country for the first time since the Maccabean revolt nearly ninety years before. Her righteous behavior and strong leadership were recognized as truly heroic for her time. Rabbinic tradition told that during her reign the grains of wheat, oats, and lentils grew to enormous size; and samples of these were kept on public display for many years to demonstrate the rewards of righteous action such as that of Queen Shulamit.[1]

A second story: In nineteenth-century Poland, in the town of Ludomir, there lived a young lady named Channah Rachel Werbermacher. From a wealthy family, she had been brought up with a good young lady's education in Torah and mitzvot, and she was promised in marriage to a fine young man. But the family was struck with tragedy when her mother died. Channah, a devout young woman, was overcome with grief. She went often to the cemetery to pray at her mother's grave, and her weeping and mourning was so intense that her father began to fear for her health and soundness of mind. The marriage plans were postponed, and, as her condition did not improve, the family eventually broke the engagement.

Events came to a head when one evening on a visit to her mother's grave Channah fell asleep weeping. She awoke in the middle of the night and, terrified, trying to find her way in the dark, stumbled into an open grave. She was found there in the morning, unconscious. She remained in a coma for some weeks.

When Channah regained consciousness, her family and neighbors soon discovered she had experienced a transformation. She began learning Chumash and midrash intensively and started teaching Torah with great spiritual depth. Women gathered in her home to hear her speak, and soon men were coming to hear her also. Soon after these events her father died, leaving her his wealth. She proceeded to buy the building next to her home for a synagogue, opened a wall between the two, and continued teaching from her own apartment, modestly behind the partition. Both men and women flocked to hear her for many years.

Although the Maid of Ludomir was admired, she was clearly something of a misfit in traditional Jewish society. While most people did not wish to stop her from teaching, many felt it would be better if she were properly married. The rabbis of the town introduced her to many suitors, but for years she accepted no offers of marriage. Finally, when she was forty—after more than twenty years of teaching—she agreed to a marriage proposal. But the marriage turned out to be bitterly unhappy and ended in divorce after only a few years.

From the time of her marriage, Channah's teaching never had the effectiveness of her earlier years. It may have been that her decision to marry was affected by an inner sense that her teaching was waning in power, or the unhappy marriage may have affected her. Her disciples diminished in number. Nevertheless, she studied assiduously and became very involved in kabbalistic thought, particularly speculations having to do with the coming of Mashiach (the Messiah). As her messianic convictions grew, she decided to move to Jerusalem. There she met a man also deeply immersed in kabbalah, and together they planned the rites and spiritual events that would, they believed, actually inaugurate the coming of Mashiach. A date and a meeting place were set for the great rites.

Unexpectedly, however, as her friend was about to leave his house for their rendezvous, a man appeared on his doorstep asking for food and a place to rest. The mitzvah of hospitality required that he postpone his meeting with Channah a little while, so he invited the guest in. Soon his guest was regaling him with stories and sharing deep mystical insights, so that he entirely forgot his messianic date with the Maid of Ludomir. The mysterious guest, the storytellers say, was Eliahu HaNavi—Elijah the Prophet, who will herald the real coming of the Messiah. After this, we hear no more of Channah Rachel.

Queen Shulamit and the Maid of Ludomir stand in the line of powerful women from the Matriarchs on down whom Jewish tradition acknowledges and extols. Yet they left no lasting dynasty or sect; their inner lives and their teachings remain unrecorded. Shulamit is given short shrift by secular historians, being remembered largely among the religious; accounts of nineteenth-century Judaism seldom mention Channah Werbermacher. Moreover, such women seem few and far between. After the times of Esther and Yehudit it is more difficult to find stories of Jewish women. From the time of the Hasmoneans down to the present, only a handful of women appear in the annals of Jewish history, most of them daughters or wives of famous rabbis.[2] Women within the tradition know of a few more—certain rebbetzins and teachers are remembered in the Chassidic sects, for example. But postbiblical history is clearly dominated by men in the roles of kings, priests, prophets, and rabbis. Are female role models like Shulamit and the Maid of Ludomir such exceptional cases that few women could follow in their footsteps, or is some other dynamic at work? Is women's influence really so small that male writers of history can easily ignore it, or does it operate in a way that it often goes unrecorded?

First of all, it is important to recognize that the dominance of men in the tradition has varied. While it is true that in all periods of Jewish history, men have outnumbered women in public leadership roles, there have been times when it was less unusual for women to rise to the fore. The most notable example is the earliest period of Israelite history, approximately a thousand years from the time of Abraham to the destruction of the First Temple, in which Bible and tradition record the names of many outstanding women. Besides the women we have considered—the four Mothers, Tamar, and Ruth (Esther and Yehudit were only slightly later)—we find stories of Zipporah and Yochoved (Moses' wife and mother, respectively), Miriam, Devorah, Hulda, and Channah. Miriam, Moses' sister, and Devorah, the famous judge and prophetess, held positions of public leadership, while Hulda was a famous teacher and prophetess consulted by King Josiah.[3]

One of the distinctive features of this period is that it was the era of prophecy, that is, when it was widely recognized that God spoke to some individuals directly, in a manner analogous to the way he spoke to Moses, to give guidance in public affairs. Prophets generally received their messages while in some kind of ecstatic state. (Moses is said to be an exception, since he could receive prophecy in normal waking consciousness.) Moreover, there were guilds or fellowships of prophets who apparently underwent some kind of training to strengthen their receptivity to divine messages.[4] Whether women formed such guilds we cannot be sure, but there is no doubt that women were prophets.

Political leadership in the early period was connected to prophecy as well. During the period of the Judges, social organization was still oriented toward family and clan, and "national" organization existed largely for the purpose of defense or conquest of territory. In times of crisis the people acknowledged temporary leaders selected by God to head all the tribes. Generally this person was regarded as having prophetic gifts in some degree—following in the footsteps of Moses. This leader, or "judge," could be a woman, as in Devorah's case.

Prophecy continued during the monarchy (eleventh to sixth century B.C.E.), and again one prominent woman is mentioned, Hulda. After the destruction of the First Temple, there were other prophets for some two hundred years, but over the period from about 500 to about 350 B.C.E., prophecy declined in practice and influence. Guidance came more and more from the Torah scholars known as the Men of the Great Assembly (Anshei Knesset Hagedolah) which was established by Ezra, the priest and scribe who led the returned exiles. Only men were part of this group. It appears that the group was dominated by priests (male only; see below) and scribes, a learned elite connected with priests and the kingly court, who were schooled in writing and interpreting Torah law.

Meanwhile, other sources of leadership had developed in the early period which, in contrast to prophecy, were totally male. The kingship, established in the eleventh century B.C.E. to replace the judges, put a man in charge of the nation, and henceforth the office was inherited among only the men of the family. Once the kingship was established, no woman led Israel for nearly a thousand years, until Shulamit.

The priesthood too was limited to men. The reasons for this are complex; certainly it was not unknown in other cultures to have priestesses serving in temples, either as associates to the men or with their own separate roles. In the Jewish context, there were probably two factors restricting women's involvement. First, most of the temple ritual revolved around animal sacrifices, which, according to tradition, had originally been performed by heads of families, the firstborn males. Later, by a decree given to Moses, the rites were handed over to the family of Levi (Moses and Aaron's family). That is to say, with greater organization and centralization of ceremonial sacrifices, one tribe was given control over all the offerings and rituals. Since men had been the "priests" in the families before, only men among the Levites were priests.

The second and equally compelling reason was the strict prohibition on impurities among those who worked with the offerings to God. These impurities ranged from physical blemishes and handicaps to—most relevant for our purposes—the prohibition on *tumah* which was associated, among other things, with discharges from the body. Since women were *tameh* during their regular menstrual periods, it is not surprising that they would be excluded from Temple service.

The significance of these developments is that once prophecy declined in relation to other forms of influence and leadership, women were effectively excluded from the public realm. Neither priest, king, nor law court official was female. By the time of the destruction of the Second Temple, there was no Jewish king, and the priesthood no longer functioned; that left the men of the law courts, who passed on the teachings of the Torah, namely, the rabbis. Rabbinic Judaism traces its heritage directly to the Men of the Great Assembly, so it is from this leadership group that we have the tradition that women are not customarily rabbis

or public interpreters of Jewish law. Nor was there any strong countervail-
ing influence from other cultures: Hellenism, which began to influence
Judaism in the fourth century B.C.E., did not encourage powerful women
and in some respects was highly misogynist. Indeed, it may have been in
reaction against Hellenism that some of the Hasmonean kings left power
in the hands of their wives: they were affirming the value of feminine
leadership. But that brief period was an exception.

Judaism is hardly alone in developing male leadership at the expense
of female: virtually all the world's major religions, and most local or
regional ones, have either restricted women's roles or excluded them
from public religious leadership. Many women today argue that this situation is a relic from the past; there is no good reason to exclude women
from religious positions, whether as ministers, priests, or rabbis. We will
not take up this debate at this point (for some comments, see chapter 8).
Here we want to examine the possible reasons why women should
appear in powerful spiritual roles in one cultural situation and not
another. For purposes of broadening our understanding, we will exclude
at first the notion that men have forcibly kept women from power. We
want to know if there is something in the nature of feminine spirituality
itself that might cause women to gravitate to certain kinds of leadership
and away from others.

The data of comparative religion suggest that women tend to be active
in and expressive of forms of religion and spirituality different from those
dominated by men. The Maid of Ludomir is one of the few clearly
documented examples in Judaism, but there are hints in the lives of many
other Jewish women that they did in fact enjoy a different kind of spirituality. In other cultures women's roles tend toward prophecy, spirit possession, shamanism, oracles, mediumship, and inspiration rather than
toward priesthood, religious kingship and other institutional offices, religious law, and textual study.[5] One could argue, of course, that the latter
fields have been so tightly controlled by men that women have not been
allowed to exercise their abilities in these areas; perhaps this will change
as women achieve greater social freedom. But for the time being, the
greater part of what we know about past religious phenomena among
women suggests that, in fact, there is a difference.

What this means is that in studying Jewish women who might be spiritual models for us, it is not enough to identify a few leading figures and
then bewail the course of history, which has excluded us for some hun-
dreds of years. Rather, we must look at the nature of spirituality itself as
it has become embedded in different forms of religious practice and religious leadership. We must learn to understand feminine spirituality on

its own terms, for only then can we begin to evaluate our present situation in Judaism with attention to its inner depths. Then we can turn again to the images of women we have examined in these first chapters and distill what is useful for us, what can inspire our lives today.

As noted above, public offices like king and priest and functions such as law and scholarship have tended to be dominated by men. Prophecy and inspiration tend to be shared by both sexes. Most scholars recognize these phenomena in familiar sociological categories: the former are established positions, "routinized," as Max Weber called them, public offices whose functioning depends very little on the personality of the individual who fills them. The second type are "charismatic," connected with personal gifts of spiritual power. Some have suggested that men dominate the official positions simply because they have obtained control of the power of appointment or inheritance. Charismatic leaders, however, are uncontrollable, appearing wherever the spiritual winds blow. As Nancy Falk and Rita Gross have written, "Religious laws and bureaucracies can dictate that only men shall be priests, but the gods choose whom they will."[6] Thus women cannot be excluded from the inspired forms of religion, even though men might like to keep them from having religious power at all.

While this scheme of understanding has points in its favor, it has some serious faults. First of all, it simply rehearses the dismal picture of patriarchal control of all significant power, with women simply fluttering their spiritual wings occasionally, to little or no effect. Further, in this view religious power is simply an aspect of social power: its political and economic functions are what count, and those functions are embedded in official positions in the socioreligious hierarchy. Conversely, official positions like king or priest have no real spiritual meaning; they are simply entry points into the realm of power understood in secular terms. But this is emphatically not the way the religious devotee experiences the people who hold such offices. Religious officials are often recognized as vessels of real spirituality, just as charismatic leaders are. Finally, this picture of religion assumes women do not choose voluntarily one kind of spirituality or another; and that by tradition, law, or outright force men keep them from exercising choice.

I think we need to face the potentially disturbing question, is it possible that some forms of spirituality are more feminine, some more masculine? Masculine and feminine themselves are certainly not exclusive traits. As Jewish mystical thought (anticipating modern psychology) has long recognized, each person has a masculine and a feminine side—as indeed does God. We must understand at the outset that any emotional, intellectual, or spiritual traits we ascribe to the "masculine" or "male" are also found in women, and "feminine" or "female" traits appear in men as well. Nevertheless, the general tendency—statistically and in most personal development—is for feminine traits to dominate the conscious life of women and masculine ones to be less developed. We may think of the masculine traits in women's psyches as assistants or consorts to the dominant feminine; and vice versa for the psychological structure of men.

To explore this area, it is best not to dichotomize spirituality in sociological terms as "official" or "charismatic," then match that dichotomy to the male-female split. We can instead think about spirituality another way, one more in accord with Jewish thought. Power in the spiritual realm comes from God, and it appears to human perception in a variety of forms. These forms make up a kind of continuum. On the one end are those forms in which the human ego virtually disappears, as in prophecy: the individual becomes the spokesperson of God and is granted a vision or foresight into the nature of things and the course of events. Often these are accompanied by physical or mental states that are observably different from normal waking consciousness—for example spirit possession or trance. At the other end are those forms in which human beings consciously and actively shape the knowledge, insight, and practice of relating to God. Examples are the intellectually oriented forms of religious law and scholarship, which seem (but appearances may deceive here) less "inspired."

Often the latter forms have grown from the former: religious scholarship develops from the study and interpretation of a unique revelation or insight, as in the Jewish tradition of Torah study. Or, as in many traditions, a regular practice, such as a meditation or rite, emerges out of a spiritual insight or direct spiritual instruction. The fact that these are derivative does not necessarily make them less "spiritual." Rather, what happens is that the conscious mind interacts with the revelation to form a cohesive and powerful new expression, one that has the potential of being accessible to more people and ultimately more effective in the world. True, these expressions may also lose their power—when the conscious mind ceases to relate to the revelation creatively and instead performs the act only by rote. Then it becomes dead ritual. But we are speaking of vital, creative spirituality.

These varied methods to call forth, gather, or strengthen the spiritual power of the human being are practiced, as rituals, in various forms and degrees by different individuals. They represent the religious work of opening the person to spiritual experience—becoming more egoless—and fusing that experience with daily reality—by using consciousness. Rituals are in fact the mode of bringing the unusual, ecstatic, or prophetic experience into a more accessible realm. Many are intentional techniques of altering consciousness, to become more open like the spiritual medium or prophet. Others discipline the mind, body, or emotions to focus on a particular kind of work or process. Still others function as small reminders to engage the individual in a relation to God even when involved in other things. And many rituals are complete systems, analogous to intellectual systems, which re-create whole worlds of thought, emotion, and action. These attempt to bring individuals and groups into a realm where, again with some openness of spirit, they can directly experience the presence of God. Finally, even the most intellectually oriented, consciously directed practices can be seen as "rituals" in an extended sense, as when Torah study is practiced by chanting the text as well as reflecting on and interpreting its meaning.

Much more can be said about these varied forms of religious expression; and in part 2 we will look at some particular examples of ritual practices. For present purposes, it is enough to get an overview, so that we can now with greater cogency ask the question, Why do women more often express themselves on the prophetic or inspired end of the spectrum rather than on the end where conscious, directed, often analytical activity is required? It is certainly not a matter of ability. And we have said that, for present purposes, we will reject the notion that men are to be blamed for keeping us away by force.

The reasons are, I believe, primarily a matter of the psychological makeup of women. First, women have strong and early tendencies to be receptive; our ability to initiate develops, as I suggested above, as an accompaniment to our feminine abilities (whether these are natural or cultural I will not debate). Because of this receptivity, we more readily let go of our ego boundaries without experiencing fear and defensiveness. Thus the egolessness of the ecstatic or prophetic kind of religion comes easily to many women. The Maid of Lubomir is an unusually vivid example of how an intense experience could bring on a transformation of consciousness that can alter a person's whole spiritual state of being, apparently in a permanent way.

Second, conscious and disciplined intellectual activity as known in our culture generally demands an objectification of one's work—a kind of "separate knowing" (in the terms used by Mary Belenky et al.), similar to what we usually call critical thinking. Not all women are comfortable with this as their predominant style; those who excel in it tend to rebel against conventional female roles.[7] Thus, a woman might be exposed to abstract learning, say in Talmud studies, but ultimately not find it satisfying because it does not call forth her capacities for relationship or involvement.[8]

Third, women tend to have less invested in hierarchical structures of power (priesthood, kingship, etc.), which often evolve along with the conscious direction of religious activity; the feminine style is to use networks more than hierarchies. We saw that when Shulamit, for example, could have taken more direct power (after her first husband's death), she chose to stay in the background and instead cultivated relationships that served her well in later years.

These factors are probably enough to explain how feminine spiritual tendencies differ from masculine without our invoking a powerful patriarchy that intentionally oppresses women. Nevertheless, it would be naive to ignore the fact that once certain structures of power and influence have developed, human egos become invested in them and will do almost anything to protect these structures from change. Priesthoods become entrenched and corrupt, armies fight wars over royal succession, and even dispassionate scholars slam doors in the faces of those who want to learn. There is no justification for forbidding women from Torah study—and fortunately most Jewish leaders recognize that now. But we must also recognize more deeply what is at stake behind male defensiveness, namely, a disturbance of the balance of male and female forces in the Jewish spiritual universe.

Most simply, this means that the balance of intuition and learning, spirit and conscious wisdom, which used to belong to both men and women in Judaism, has been disturbed. Men occupied positions of power, and over the centuries some came to rely on those positions—rather than on their own spiritual development—as a source of strength. At the same time, women faded into the background, and strong, individualized female models disappeared from public memory. Already in the stories of Esther and Yehudit one can detect a romanticizing of what Aviva Cantor has called the "altruistic/assertive" woman, an idealization that, unlike earlier biblical portrayals, overlooks a woman's faults.[9] Similarly, Rachel Adler has complained that the righteous women of later tradition seem to lack the individuality, the idiosyncratic features, of their male counterparts; they appear one after another as selfless servants of others.[10] While service to others is always an admired trait in Judaism, for men as well as women, the sense of purpose and destiny that one finds in earlier portrayals has diminished.

Knowing our heritage gives us a background of strength. But we also see that our strengths have taken second place to those of men, and that, ultimately, we have been institutionalized out of positions of influence. To reestablish ourselves—and indeed the balance of Jewish life as a whole—we must ask ourselves, how can we nourish our own spirituality, develop our own spiritual strength? For it is only by knowing and acting on our deep inner strength that we can, individually and collectively, contribute to bringing the world to a higher level. We must affirm what comes naturally to us while we also grow in other areas. This is the way that our leadership can be clear, focused, and truly feminine.

The archetypal models we have looked at give us some hints as to the nature of Jewish women's spirituality as seen through the lenses of our tradition. We can list here in abbreviated form some of the characteristics of women in the stories of this and earlier chapters—stories of Sarah and the other mothers, of Ruth, Tamar, Esther, Yehudit, Shulamit, and the Maid of Lubomir.

prophetic/inspired

future oriented, with a sense of history and destiny

focused on real-life experience (e.g., childbirth) and intimate relations (family and kin)

having own distinctive relationship to God

sexually/sensually based sense of holiness

sense of power hidden beneath the surface

risk taking, life saving, redemptive

Many of the characteristics listed have to do with what we might call the earthly—or as feminist theologians put it, the "immanental"—orientation of the feminine. The growth and development of our spirituality comes in daily, even biological, life as much as in extraordinary experiences. Childbirth is the archetypal expression of this, as in Sarah's expression of joyful faith, or, as Psalm 113 says, "[God] turns the barren woman into a joyful mother of children." Through giving birth and nurturing, a woman learns and grows in new ways.[11] Similarly, the emphasis on the sexuality of women, as with Tamar or Yehudit, expresses a strong sense of the holiness of embodiment, of being in a body. The realm of family relations is revelatory, particularly for all the matriarchs, who show us the potential for significant action in relationships. In all our examples, the woman is responsible for saving and enriching life. And, in the process, the woman develops her own relationship with God, as did Rachel and Leah. It is in the struggles and victories of daily life, both her inner life and her external activities, that women's spiritual strengths emerge. This suggests that the feminine spiritual archetype is not necessarily one clear role—like a young man's single-minded career choice (though this too may be changing in today's world), or like the official roles of priest, king, or rabbi. Rather, it is a path of development that takes the matter of life as it comes and fashions it, bit by bit, into the clarity of purpose and faith that motivated a Yehudit or a Ruth.

Moreover, our examples show that extraordinary consciousness can develop in the midst of this ordinary life. The prophetic orientation we saw in Sarah and many others, that intuition of destiny, is part of what we called the prophetic end of the spectrum of spirituality that has been known to women cross-culturally. The models we have seen so far, however, give us no clues as to how women developed that ability. While it may come naturally to some degree, or appear in psychological crisis as with Channah Werbermacher, we need to know more about this. The Jewish mystical traditions offer some perspective; and Torah study itself is recommended for developing clarity of mind, as we will see in chapter 6. But this is an area open to more study and exploration.

The images of women we discussed in chapters 1 and 2 exemplify a dynamic between the prophetic and the ordinary, the insight of a higher consciousness and the work of everyday life. In this light the Maid of Ludomir is both a positive and a negative model. On the one hand, she reminds us of the starting point of it all: the deep unconscious connection with God that brings forth inspiration. It is no accident that it was the death of her mother, opening the unconscious connection with the feminine, that started her on her path. But on the other hand, it was no accident either that her unhappy marriage coincided with the decline of her powers and set her on a path that was ultimately fruitless. Channah had become a vessel for pure Torah, inspired teaching; and she incorporated in her later life the great yearning for redemption, for the Messiah, for return to Jerusalem and the perfection of the world that has inspired all of Judaism. But she apparently came to believe that redemption could be accomplished through the power of mind and spirit alone. She had not learned the lessons of the Mothers, that we must work out our spirituality in contact with the world, in relation to people.

Queen Shulamit was at the other extreme, occupying the official position of ruler. From her support of the Pharisees under all conditions, we know her to have been deeply religious; but we have no hint of what role her piety played in her inner life. She followed precepts that were central to pharisaic teaching: to establish justice and pursue peace. She sought no central role. Whether for her own safety or because of her personal preference, she did not seek to rule alone after Aristobulus died, but married his brother so that he could take the throne. Nevertheless, over the next thirty years, she cultivated relationships and that allowed her to reign in peace in her old age and exemplified a life-style that attracted the admiration of the people. Thus, she is remembered for her dedication and for her mastery of the arts of peace, not for her charisma. Shulamit was very much a woman of practical wisdom.

If these examples are representative, women of postbiblical times tended to take one of two directions: The more usual was a life of relationship and involvement in family, community, and world, under the guidance of tradition. Less common was the Maid of Ludomir's path: the life of religious ecstasy that left her largely alone. Yet the leading models presented to us in earlier tradition bring together a combination of these characteristics. They acted in the practical realm: actions like Sarah's and Rivkah's that shaped the original Jewish families, like Tamar's and Ruth's that extended the heritage, like Esther's and Yehudit's that saved innumerable lives in times of deep crisis. Yet they also were models of insight, inner knowledge, deep and direct connection with God, at times approaching the level of prophecy.

What does this mean for us? Certainly, this world of action is where most of us live, not in the realms of kabbalah, but in the midst of work and family and community. Yet we also know that full development means paying attention to our inner lives. For some of us combining these two may mean taking on a spiritual "career choice" as men have often done; but for many or even most women it likely will not. The women of our tradition attest that spirituality can develop in anyone from a great queen to a poor outsider. We operate in a different way from men; and we can all be, in a sense, priestesses of a holy sanctuary.

What exactly is this practice, this priestess work? Shulamit provides a good example for a beginning: she surrounded herself with wise teachers. She learned from them the foundation, the mitzvot (commandments) of Judaism. With this grounding, we can move into higher levels of consciousness that emerge from several interrelated features of Jewish life: learning of Torah; deeper practice and insight into the ritual life of Judaism; self-development through growth in ethical consciousness; and prayer and meditation to develop our inner connection with God.

In the next part, we will discuss a few aspects of Jewish ritual life that are especially relevant to women. We will be looking first at those dimensions which are connected with direct action in our ordinary lives. Without becoming queens or rabbis, we have the opportunity to refine our consciousness and at the same time transform the world through our actions and intentions. We will go on to look at the possibilities of deeper individual inner work. Careful attention to all these areas reveals to us, I believe, the essence of the Jewish spiritual path and the opening to a deeper and richer life as women.

Part 2

THOUGHT, SPEECH, ACTION

She turned to call the mists. . . .
She drew a deep breath,
charging herself for the magical act,
knowing she must concentrate all her strength. . . .
Up went her arms into the arch of the sky;
down, with the mists following
the sweep of her trailing sleeves.
Mist and silence hung dark around them. *
Avalon.

She touched the flame to each light, one by one,
closed her eyes,
focusing inwardly,
gathering her loved ones with her. . . .
She drew a deep breath,
concentrating all her strength. . . .
Raised her hands gently, powerfully,
three circles
bringing the light toward her,
that distant light, essence of light,
hidden since the dawn of time,
its softness suddenly filled her home.
Shabbat.

Rituals have fascinated anthropologists, psychologists, and students of religion for decades. Many explanations have been proposed of their power and endurance. Less than a century ago, many thought that rituals were obsolete in the face of science. Yet today rites and ceremonies are enjoying a renaissance. Rituals of rebirth in psychotherapy, rituals of magic in new cults, rituals of prayer for people who had long ago given up belief in God—these and more one can find among people of any social group or class. In Judaism too individuals who otherwise are alienated from traditional religion find pleasure and satisfaction in attending some kind of Shabbat or holiday celebration; people who will not attend a synagogue form their own informal groups to celebrate the rituals.

The specialness of ritual is twofold: first, it is not mere thought or speech but a concrete, usually tangible, reality that is taken up and con-

---

* Marion Zimmer Bradley, *The Mists of Avalon* (New York: Ballantine Books, 1982), pp. 142–43.

sciously transformed in a dramatic context. Lighting Shabbat candles or a Chanukkah menorah is not like other candlelighting. A sukkah is an inhabitable space that is also a fantasy house. In ritual, things of this world are made to be like things from another world, another time and space. Yet at the same time one often feels more attuned to the present when participating in a ritual than in one's normal course of life.

Second, rituals often are connected to a different state of consciousness in those who perform them. Some of this consciousness is created by the person's intention: I intend that my prayer should open my heart to God. Often, in addition, there are specific physical and mental acts that create an unusual state of mind and body: fasting, intense activity, group participation, music, dancing, repetition of movements or words, meditation. The changes are subtle and often untraceable. They work, however, in breaking down the hypnotic force of everyday consciousness and allowing, hopefully, some deeper perception or some more intense energy to break through.

The reason most scholarly explanations of ritual have not been satisfactory is that those explaining do not usually believe that the transformation experienced in ritual is real. The world created, the drama performed, is to the observer simply an aesthetic object. But to the person inside the ritual, whose consciousness is being changed in the very same acts that create the drama, the reality is unquestionable. Acts, thoughts, emotions become possible that were not possible before. It may look like psychological sleight of hand, but no: something from another "world," another level, has indeed slipped in, been allowed into our ordinary world. Once this is experienced, nothing can quite be the same again.

I quoted the passage from *The Mists of Avalon* to suggest that we, like the female heroines of that story, can be vessels—priestesses, so to speak—of these transformations. We saw in the last chapter that women often steer away from activities that separate them from concrete experience, that are merely abstract. We prefer to stay close to people and things, knowing the details, being involved rather than being observers or manipulators from outside. For this reason ritual is often more congenial than abstract study of spiritual matters. In addition, we saw that women can lose or loosen their ego boundaries to be open to processes that come from other levels of consciousness, other levels of reality. Our receptivity is great, and we are easily affected by practices that shift our consciousness. (This may be the reason that the sages held that women are more spiritual than men, more easily focused inward, and less in need of specific techniques to train their spirituality.)

As women, then, we are in a privileged position in opening the channels of the world to the divine flow. At the beginning we may not see what is the direct benefit to the world of all the rituals we can perform. It is tempting to push aside davening and run to a political action meeting or sign up for a Saturday class on economic theories that will end poverty. These may be valuable actions, but we must learn to think twice before we relegate ritual practice to second priority. What happens through our Jewish practice is nothing less than a realignment of the world, preparing the world to accept goodness and truth that have never before been revealed. Women are spiritual midwives in rebirthing the world. Just how is a mystery; but this too is revealed to us, piece by piece, as we do the work itself.

CHAPTER 4

Rhythms of Jewish Life

To everything there is a season.
In the play of love and mourning,
laughter and solemnity,
God hides and reappears,
and so do we.

The life in which we sanctify the world revolves around what in Judaism are called the *mitzvot*, usually translated "commandments." Many of these have to do with rituals, the ceremonial acts by which we consecrate our time, our space, our relationships, our passages through life. The details of the mitzvot, how to do them and whatever explanations may be attached to them, are the subject of much discussion in Torah and rabbinic literature. Yet there is an important dimension of living the *mitzvot* that one does not always encounter on first meeting, namely, what is called the *kavannah*, the "intention" that accompanies the act. Kavannah or intention is, as Rabbi Adin Steinsaltz puts it, the "subjective meaning to the *mitzvah* in the mind of the doer at the moment when he carries it out."[1] This aspect of the work of ritual (or other kinds of mitzvot) is significant because the intention, the thought and general orientation we bring to the mitzvah, can greatly enhance our awareness of God and of our purpose in life, and can affect the quality of the act itself.

Rabbi Steinsaltz points out that there are different kinds of kavannot. First, we perform a mitzvah with the awareness that we are doing just that: doing what God asks of us, with a desire to connect to God. In addition, there are various kinds of "mystical and symbolic" kavannot that, he says, "are essentially forms of communion with the Divine, but are active and affective rather than intellectual or abstract. The meditation [on these] lends the performance of the *mitzvah*, the outward physical act, a depth and warmth of feeling and a spiritual exaltation."[2] As workers in a holy sanctuary, we want to bring such warmth into our lives, not simply perform rote actions. This is how our conscious minds can bring us in touch with the deeper, unconscious significance encoded in the rituals.

When we seek to develop this kind of consciousness in ways that also will connect us with our femininity, we find that Jewish tradition offers great delights. The very fabric of Jewish life, established by the rhythms of seasons and festivals, is richly interwoven with feminine themes. A friend and early teacher once remarked to me, "Judaism is a feminine religion with a patriarchal veneer." Nowhere is this more true than in the round of seasonal rituals. Indeed, one of the most direct ways of deepening our understanding of Jewish life is to look at Shabbat and the holidays and how they incorporate what we might call the feminine principle.

Rituals that have to do with time are one of the most fascinating and mysterious of mitzvot. When we perform, with kavannah, a ritual that inaugurates a festive day, we have the possibility of entering into new dimensions of time. Each time, each season, each year, each period of history has its own quality of energy, its own distinctive subtle traits. As we incorporate even a little of the kavannah associated with the day or season, the effect is twofold: our experience changes, and we become channels for that energy to affect our part of the world. We learn, for example, that God created a special quality of rest, *menuchah*, which is revealed on every seventh day; when we observe Shabbat, we can experience that quality of being.

The same is true of the Yomim Tovim, the holidays—as we read in the prayers, "times for rejoicing, holidays and seasons for happiness." Many of the Jewish holidays partake of two kinds of energy: that of the season of the year where they fall—spring, fall harvest, and so on—and that of the events of Jewish history and tradition they commemmorate. There is an energy associated with spring, and at Pesach that quality is interwoven with the qualities of God that were revealed to the Jewish people during the Exodus from Egypt. (Indeed, all the holidays as well as Shabbat have some taste of the Exodus, in addition to whatever other qualities they have. We say in every kiddush before the celebratory evening meal that it is "in memory of the going out from Egypt.") Shavuot is a harvest holiday, and also the time of the giving of the Torah; and so on through the year. With this in mind, we can follow the days of celebration around the calendar and explore their various dimensions.

The center of Jewish life is, of course, Shabbat. We count our days from Shabbat and to Shabbat and organize our lives around it. An acquaintance once remarked, "Some of these other groups seem so much better organized than we are. But I finally recognized that they have much more time to spend on meetings, telephone, and the rest because their main purpose is political organization. Our main purpose is Shabbat and the holidays—we have to stretch to have time for anything else!" She spoke a great truth: as Jews, we must do in six days what others do in seven; in addition, we spend time doing special things to prepare ourselves for Shabbat.

If one prepares for it and sets the day aside as holy, the blessings of Shabbat pour out in remarkable ways. At the same time, the more complete the preparation, the more one's consciousness changes, and the more receptive one can be. Shabbat is a day of being, not becoming, so we need to put away all those bits of life that involve creating, finishing, planning, in order to have a mind free of past and future. For six days we are active co-creators of the world with God; on the seventh, we enter with God into a receptive frame. And, although God is always masculine and feminine and beyond either of these, we experience God on Shabbat as the feminine, the Queen.[3]

The queen, the *kalla* or bride, enters the home and the synagogue on Friday night, to the sweet and joyous melodies of "L'cha Dodi": "Come, my beloved, to greet the bride, to welcome the face of Shabbat!" The whole Jewish people are urged to rise up, shake off the dust of worry and discontent, and join in rejoicing; for when the Shabbat Queen arrives, we glimpse the promise of messianic times. The legends tell us that a male prophet, Elijah, will announce the coming of a male king, the Mashiach (Messiah), a descendant of David. But the spirit of the times will be like the spirit of Shabbat in its freshness: the joyous feminine represented by the bride.

We read at the Shabbat table—sometimes it is read (or sung) only by the head of the household, sometimes by men, sometimes by all—the famous "woman of valor" passage from the end of the book of Proverbs. It is often taken as a tribute to the woman of the house; but it is also a proclamation of the feminine as Israel itself, the Jewish people with their collective feminine soul, the Shekhinah. The passage invokes many feminine themes:

Who can find a woman of excellence?
> Her value is far greater than gems.
>> . . .
Like the merchant ships she brings food from afar.
She rises while it is night,
> gives food to her household
> and sets out the tasks for her maids.
She considers a field and buys it;
From her earnings she plants a vineyard.
> . . . Her lamp does not go out at night.
She holds out her hands to the poor,
> and extends her hands to the destitute . . .
She makes her own tapestries;
> her garments are of fine linen and purple . . .
Strength and dignity are her garb;
> she looks smilingly to the future.
She opens her mouth with wisdom,
> and the teaching of kindness is on her tongue.
She watches the conduct of her household
> and does not eat the bread of idleness.
Her children rise and acclaim her;
> her husband also, and praises her:
Many daughters have done worthily,
> but you surpass them all.
Charm is deceptive, beauty is vain—
> the Godfearing woman is to be praised.
Give her praise for her accomplishments,
> and let her deeds laud her at the gates.

The woman is praised for her part in the continuing work of creation: providing, planting, caring and nurturing, compassion, and providing for the future. Deeply involved in the daily life of family, community, and world, she creates bounty and plenitude. Always active, weaving and moving, in a vigorous beauty that comes from inner strength, she also speaks and teaches wisdom to those around her.[4]

Each Shabbat evening we remind ourselves that these forces are what sustain us, have sustained us throughout the week of activity, and now join together in a special quality of rest. In the Shabbat davening according to the Nusach Ari, which includes some of the mystical kavannot of the great Isaac Luria, we say that She, the Shekhinah, the divine force manifest in this world, "unites below into the mystery of oneness." "Her countenance is irradiated with the holy supernal light, and she crowns herself here below with the holy people, all of whom are crowned with new souls."[5] This is the "Shabbat Queen," the divine and deeply feminine forces of the world for whom we, the Jewish people, are the crown. In the Shabbat evening service we pray that "all Israel who sanctify Your name will rest on her [*vah*]"; and we call the evening meal "the meal of the holy *Chakal Tapuchin*," a feminine divine manifestation, and the masculine forces "come to join her in the meal."[6] Thus, the sense of the feminine, queenly presence continues throughout Shabbat evening.

Although all of Shabbat is considered feminine, it is noteworthy that the prayer in the Amidah referred to above changes as the day progresses. The next morning, in the Shacharit and Musaf services, we pray "may all Israel who sanctify your name rest on him [*vo*]," while at Mincha we ask that God grant us holy Shabbat days, and "may all Israel who sanctify your Name rest on them [*vam*]." The second and third meals are offered by the masculine forces, and "she" comes to join them. We have a hint here of a shift of energy, to the masculine in the morning and the union of the two in the afternoon as Shabbat comes to a harmonious close. This dynamic is crucial to a sense of the rhythm of Jewish life, and we will see it again in the cycle of the holiday seasons discussed below.

Shabbat represents the feminine in powerful form, the Shekhinah manifest in her unity. The whole concept of the Shekhinah, the divine Presence in the world, has become very important in Jewish mysticism.[7] It suggests that insofar as we know God's presence in the world—in the forces of nature, in the ordinary course of our own lives—we know it as feminine. The Shekhinah was manifest in the clouds of glory covering the Israelites traveling in the desert; she was the radiance experienced in the Holy Temple in Jerusalem. After the destruction of the Temple and the exile of the Jewish people, the Shekhinah went into exile as well. Fragmented and scattered, she is difficult to perceive; but she is with us, like Rachel yearning and weeping, even in our alienated state. When we reunify the Jewish people, we will once more be able to experience, clearly and powerfully, the Shekhinah in our daily life. In the meantime, we can still experience the powerful impact of her unity on Shabbat. And Shabbat is the direct feminine connection with God.

Another of the strongly feminine holidays is Rosh Chodesh, or the New Moon, which is celebrated one or two days each month. This ancient holy day, on which it was customary to go and hear the teaching of Torah, is considered a holiday special to women. This should not suprise us: in many cultures the moon has often been associated with women, its changing phases analogous to our monthly menstrual cycles. Its diffuse, mysterious light, its harmony with the darkness, and its changes archetypally represent the feminine in the symbolism of the psyche.

In Jewish tradition the midrash tells us that the day was given over to women as a reward for their devotion to God in the episode of the golden calf. According to the story, after Moses had disappeared on Mount Sinai for forty days, the "mixed multitude" who had come out of Egypt with the Hebrew slaves demanded a figure of a god so that they could worship the god who had brought them out of Egypt. The Jewish men, of all the tribes except Moses' own tribe Levi, supported their request and gave over all the gold they had brought out of Egypt to Moses' brother Aaron, the high priest, to be melted down and made into a golden calf. The women refused. They knew that although Moses was gone, his "light" was hidden only temporarily, like the moon in its dark phase. Soon he would return and lead them onward. As a reward for their faith and loyalty, they were given a special holiday, Rosh Chodesh.

The custom has been for women to treat Rosh Chodesh as a kind of half holiday: we do not refrain from all work, but avoid hard labor—classically, doing laundry (which certainly used to be backbreaking) and other difficult chores. Many women have the custom of dressing up for the holiday or preparing some kind of special dish for the evening meal. Women's groups often set aside a Rosh Chodesh evening for a special gathering—to learn together, hear a guest speaker, or sing and dance.

Rosh Chodesh is observed by men too via changes in the Shemoneh Esreh prayers and grace after meals, the singing of half-Hallel, and a special reading from the Torah scroll. Most of all, however, Rosh Chodesh guides the whole Jewish year: we operate on a primarily lunar calendar. This calendar is adjusted to fit the solar cycle by adding a thirteenth lunar month every second or third year, so that the holidays keep their approximate place in the solar seasons (Pesach staying in the spring, Sukkot in the fall, etc.). But the whole structure of the year has a lunar—which is to say a feminine—foundation. We might say that God honored the feminine dimension of the created universe by giving the moon the rulership of our structure of time.

The command to proclaim the appearance of the New Moon was the first command given to the Jewish people in Egypt. They were to announce the New Moon of Nisan, and henceforth that month would be the first of the months. From that day they would be able to count to the tenth, when each family was to take out a lamb from the flock, and the fourteenth, when they were to sacrifice the lamb and eat it—the first Passover meal. The New Moon of Nisan thus inaugurates the counting of months, beginning with the month of the great redemption. Although we also have a new year celebration six months later, we can best see the feminine elements in the structure of the year by starting from Nisan: from this lunar month begins a special cycle of the human-divine relationship.

One of the most important kavannot through which Jewish mystics have grasped Jewish life is to see it as a series of moments in the relationship between God and Israel, on the model of a bride and groom. We have seen already, in discussing Shabbat, that the feminine expression is followed by the masculine, then the union of the two. In the larger scheme, the bride is Israel on the human side; the groom is God, the divine.[8] Their courtship begins in the month of Nisan, when God takes his beloved out from slavery, where her beauty had been hidden from the world. In celebration of this aspect of the Exodus, we sing at Pesach the *Shir HaShirim*, the Song of Songs, as the biblical book that accompanies the holiday. This beautiful love poem speaks of the love between a man and woman, their desire for each other, their separation and union—a moving accompaniment to the betrothal, the first pledge of love, between Israel and God. The images of woman in the book are powerful as well; as Arthur Waskow has noted, the song celebrates "a mode of spirituality that flows from the life-experience of women."[9]

Women are quite prominent in the midrashic stories about Pesach. Tradition tells us that God performed the redemption from Egypt because of the merit of the Jewish women. Their honorable actions proved to him that the people deserved to be redeemed. The chief Hebrew midwives, known in the Bible as Shifrah and Puah (the midrash says that their Hebrew names were Yochoved and Miriam, Moses' mother and sister), refused to assist Pharaoh in his wicked plan to kill all the newborn babies. The Torah reports that they told him, "The Hebrew women are not like the Egyptian women; when they go into labor, they give birth before the midwife can get to them" (Exod. 1:19). Thus they were unable to kill the baby boys immediately as he had commanded. The midrash adds that they hid babies in special caves and other places, and the infants were miraculously fed.

A wonderful story is told about Miriam, Moses' sister, before Moses was born. Her father, Amram, had become very downhearted about the situation of the Jewish slaves. In despair he declared that he would bring no more babies into this world and divorced Yochoved. Miriam went to him and said, "You are worse than Pharaoh! The king is trying to kill only the boys—you want to do away with the girls too!" He recognized the truth of what she was saying and decided to remarry Yochoved. Soon after, Moses was born, who was destined to lead the people to freedom.

Part of the "affliction" of the hard labor in Egypt was its disruption of family life, in particular, relations between husband and wife. But, the midrash says, the women overcame that by stealing quietly out to the fields where the men slept not only to bring them food, but also dressed in their finest clothes and made up to be attractive to them, so that, despite the men's exhaustion, their relations would continue. They polished pieces of copper into mirrors so that they could make themselves attractive. For this God later rewarded them when the Mishkan was built, by having these mirrors made into the washing vessel for the priests. Moses objected to this plan, seeing the mirrors as simply utensils of vanity. But God insisted: these mirrors were used with holy intent, for the very survival of the Jewish people. We see here echoes of the stories of chapter 2: part of woman's power is her sexuality, here used also to help save Jewish lives.

These midrashic embellishments to the story of the Exodus emphasize how potent is the motif of the union of man and woman in Jewish tradition. Egypt, which is often taken as a symbol of descent into materialism and hedonism—the "fleshpots" of Egypt, the rich delicacies available there—distracted the Hebrew slaves from what was most holy, the relation of husband and wife. We might say that in Egypt the Jewish women corrected Eve's sin of eating the forbidden fruit: ignoring the temptations of Egypt's rich cuisine, they focused on building families.

In this light too it is clear how the metaphor of male-female union became a mode of understanding the redemption itself: a new relationship between the people and God was formed, the relationship not of father to son ("Jacob is my firstborn son") but of lover to beloved. The midrash reflects the people's experience of the importance of the male-female bond in the family. Thus, from the parent-child stage of the Abrahamitic period, the Jewish people moved to a mature relationship, that of wife to husband.

The next major holiday, Shavuot, becomes another stage in the relationship: the written marriage contract, or ketubah, symbolized in the tablets containing the Ten Commandments given to the Jews on Mount Sinai. The Torah is the binding document, the legal aspect of the relationship. Here the feminine side is rather subdued, as in Jewish legal practice itself: the man gives the ketubah as his promise to the woman, for her security and protection. But in the giving of the Torah at Sinai, the midrash stresses that the women were very significant recipients. The Torah states that Moses was told to "speak to the households of Jacob, and say to the children of Israel." The "households," says the midrash, were the women; the "b'nei Yisroel" the men. The Torah was given first to women, because God knew they had to be the primary guardians of the agreement. Moreover, the difference in the command, "speak" rather than "say," means that God told Moses to use a soft tone and kind voice—for this is how a man should speak to a woman. To the men he should be stricter and more commanding.

We have already mentioned another principal feminine aspect of Shavuot: the book read to accompany the holiday is the book of Ruth. We saw that Ruth, while modest, was a bold and decisive woman, willing to take risks to create the kind of life she believed in. In the context of Shavuot, Ruth represents the total dedication with which a Jew approaches the marriage contract with God. "Where you go, I will go, . . . your people will be my people, and your God, my God." The unquestioning devotion she offered to Naomi, her mother-in-law, is the model here—a woman binding herself to a kind of mother and spiritual guide. The gentleness between them, the sense of respect from younger to older, concern from older to younger, and their absolute mutual support—each doing her part according to her ability—compose a delicate picture of the relation of the Jewish people to God. For, at the time of Shavuot, every Jew dedicates herself again to Torah, becomes in effect a convert, like Ruth, like the whole Jewish people at Sinai thirty-three hundred years ago. The book of Ruth softens the hierarchical, masculine feeling of the giving of commandments or writing of a legal contract, offering us a genuinely feminine perspective on marriage bonds, which are the model for human beings' relationship to God. It is not the relationship between Ruth and Boaz that is the model here, but Ruth's devotion to Naomi. As women bond to each other, so we enter into our marriage commitment to God.

Thus a partnership is established at Shavuot between God and the Jewish people. But before the marriage can be consummated, as it were, trouble appears on the horizon: the wife is unfaithful. The incident is that of the golden calf, described above. Although the women did not support the worshiping of the calf, the Jewish people, as the "woman" betrothed to God, turned aside from their true love to follow an idolatrous temptation. This act of infidelity took place in the month of Tammuz. The next unhappy event, according to tradition, was on the ninth of Av a year later: the spies who had been sent to Canaan brought back a mixed report, and the people, frightened of the difficult wars they might have to fight, backed off from the plan to cross over into the promised land. Subsequently this was the date on which both the First and Second Temple were destroyed and, among other things, the date of the expulsion of the Jews from Spain. Midsummer became a time of tragedy, sadness, heartbreak. We can see here a subtle change in the energies of the universe, in the heat of high summer symbolized by broken relationships, wars, separation, violation of what is holy.[10] Nature reflects that shift, but what we see in nature mirrors spiritual reality on a higher plane. Thus today, because of many tragic events of the season recorded in tradition and history, Jews are warned to be cautious and circumspect during the "three weeks" from the seventeenth of Tammuz to the ninth of Av.

Av is followed by Elul, when Moses ascended the mountain again, begging forgiveness from God on behalf of the Jewish people. God is especially close during this time: the king, according to the mystical teachings, is walking in the field among his people, and we can approach him like a friend. We are preparing our *tshuvah*, our return to God, our return to our deepest selves, which will culminate in Rosh Hashanah. The Hebrew letters for Elul—*aleph, lamed, vav, lamed,* are an acronym for a verse from the Song of Songs: *ani l'dodi v'dodi li*—"I am my beloved's, and my beloved is mine"—again echoing the theme that nearness to God is like the closeness of two lovers.

Rosh Hashanah is known by several names besides the day of the "new year." One is Yom Hazikaron, the day of remembering. On the first day of Rosh Hashanah, we read in the synagogue two passages about God's remembering, and in both cases they are about women. "And God remembered Sarah," and gave her a son, Isaac; and in the Haftarah, "God remembered Channah," answering her prayers by giving her a child, Shmuel the prophet. Many other remembrances are mentioned on Rosh Hashanah, but it is very much to the point that the theme is told first of all in the stories of two women. Originally, Sarah had accepted her childlessness and had given her maid Hagar to Abraham as a concubine. But this had caused trouble in the household, and Hagar was sent away. An angel told her to return and promised her that her son would be the ancestor of a great nation; but at this point God also promised Abraham that Sarah would become pregnant. The entire episode communicates God's continual caring and watching over the events on earth. More particularly, it was in response to Sarah's distress over her changed relationship with Hagar that the promise came to her.

We have not yet met Channah, but, as we will see in the next chapter, her heartfelt prayer also expressed her great distress. Her situation was much like Rachel's: she was greatly loved by her husband, Elkanah, but she was childless. Her co-wife, Pnina, continually reminded her of her troubles. She promised that if she could have a son, she would dedicate him to God as a *nazir* and bring him to the temple to learn with the priests. God remembered Channah, giving her Shmuel, who was to be one of the great judges and prophets of Jewish history, leading the Jewish people himself and then establishing the kingship of Saul and then David.

There are many other times that God is said to have "remembered" the Jewish people or specific individuals. It is not, of course, as if God could literally "forget." Rather, the time of remembering is the time of a shift in destiny. The significance of the examples of the two women is that this came about from a renewed commitment on their part: Sarah had expressed her commitment by offering Hagar to Abraham so that he could have a child, Channah by vowing to give her child to be raised by the Temple priests. God's response was to alter their destiny entirely. In this context it is no accident that in the Haftarah reading for the second day, from the prophet Jeremiah, another woman is mentioned: Rachel, weeping for her children. The promise is that as we renew our commitment, God will fulfill her hopes and prayers, returning us to our land and the life that we yearn for. In a number of ways, then, it is women who signal the renewal of life and hope and the potential shift in our lives that comes with each new year.

Other aspects of Rosh Hashanah should be mentioned briefly here, although they are not particularly feminine. The day is also Yom HaTruah, the day of the sounding of the shofar—an experience powerful and beloved to the people for centuries. The shofar recalls the giving of the Torah, when trumpet sounds were heard on Mount Sinai, and, made from a ram's horn, it recalls Abraham and Isaac. Thus it echoes deep in Jewish history. In the psyche it is like an implement of a shaman, an instrument from the animal world that augurs power and strength, calling us back to our inner depths. The mitzvah of hearing the shofar was not originally obligatory for women, but, because women have universally taken it on, it is now considered a mitzvah for us as well as for men. At the same time, Rosh Hashanah expresses *Malkhut*, "kingship," which is also equivalent to the Shekhinah, the feminine aspect of God. In accepting God as our king, we the Jewish people express our consent to God as ruler of the universe. We acknowledge that the creative energy that transcends the universe, from which everything came, is connected to the depths within ourselves, the inner power that cannot be expressed in words.

Rosh Hashanah also inaugurates the ten Days of Awe, the intense time of introspection and self-evaluation that we call *tshuvah*, returning to God. The culmination is, of course, Yom Kippur. The midrash tells us that it was on Yom Kippur that Moses returned from Mount Sinai with the second set of tablets, announcing God's complete forgiveness. The relationship between God and the Jewish people was restored to its original purity. Thus Yom Kippur, despite its solemn prayers, is also a day of great joy. In an earlier period, the day after Yom Kippur was a great festive day on which the women danced in their fine garments, and many matches were made. Mystically speaking, the "marriage" between God and the Jewish people is reaffirmed, with a rewritten "contract," and then consummated a few days later at Sukkot—which, like Pesach, when the courtship began, falls on a full moon.

The sukkah is a kind of chupah, a marriage canopy, as well as symbolizing the huts the Israelites inhabited in their desert travels. Indeed, when one eats and (as some have the custom) sleeps in a festive sukkah, it becomes a kind of dream house—one brings to it none of the cares and worries of every day, only the joyous feelings of Yom Tov. This holiday is the "season of our rejoicing," so the mood is much like a wedding. The six months from Pesach to Sukkos thus replicate the movements of a love relationship, from romance to betrothal, commitment and alienation, renewed commitment, reconciliation, union and rejoicing.

During the cycle of these major holidays, the feminine is engaged in a kind of dance—the Shekhinah or feminine Presence in the world with the more distant masculine aspect of God. In the next six months the tempo and tone shift somewhat. Major biblical and agricultural holidays are absent, and instead we have two popular rabbinically established holidays, Chanukkah and Purim. One might expect that since these are not rooted in the most ancient layer of Jewish history, where we have seen that women are fairly prominent, these would be masculinized holidays. But the contrary is true. The feminine, which is in so many traditions associated with darkness, winter, and the hidden potential of things, emerged here in Judaism as well. The stories associated with the two holidays involve, historically, both men and women, but in popular tradition they are often considered a "tribute to women."[11] Certainly that is true of Purim, as we have seen already with the story of Esther. In many respects it is true of Chanukkah as well.

Traditionally, Chanukkah celebrates a military victory and a miracle— the "miracle of the oil"—associated with the rededication of the Temple.

(Chanukkah literally means "dedication.") But legends surrounding the events that led to the Maccabean revolt involve women—for example, the incident that tradition tells us incited Judas Maccabee to rally his men for war. A daughter of Matthiahu, enraged at the prohibition of circumcision, led a group of mothers of infant boys to the top of the city walls. There, in full view of the people, they circumcised their children then leaped to their deaths. Another famous incident occurred when soldiers, enforcing King Antiochus's religious persecution, rounded up crowds of people and demanded that they bow down to an idol. When the soldiers came to Channah and her family of seven sons, all refused to bow down. The soldiers took the sons, one by one, and killed them right in front of their mother. Each time, they offered to spare the life of the next one if she would bow down; each time she refused. Even the youngest went bravely to his death, and then they killed Channah herself.

The moral of the stories is not merely that the women were willing to sacrifice themselves for the cause but that they led and inspired the whole people to uphold their Jewish faith and practice in the face of persecution. Like Esther and Yehudit in their times, they emerged from their usual private lives into the public domain when the situation called for it—in this case in dramatic self-sacrifice that challenged and inspired the rest of the people to overthrow the hated Hellenistic government. As we have already pointed out, we read the story of Yehudit at Chanukkah, even though the events on which it is based took place long before the Maccabean era, and the story of Esther at Purim. Each story echoes the other: the tales of courageous women whose actions molded the history of the Jewish people.

Other themes of Chanukkah are suggestive of the feminine. The Chanukkah celebration is focused in the home, emphasizing family togetherness and enacting the themes of rededication and renewal. Like most Jewish holidays, it has a seasonal dimension suggesting the natural world: the renewal of the lighting of the menorah in the Temple, symbolized by lighting candles each of the eight nights of the holiday, corresponds to the renewal of light at the winter solstice—suggested by the fact that we light an increasing number of lights each night.

One develops a sense of the winter holidays as different in quality from the cycle from spring to fall. They are oriented more toward home and children; even though there is a public reading of Megillat Esther on Purim, it is done lightly and with much festive entertainment for the children (and the adults, expressing the child within). Chanukkah and Purim both commemorate serious events, but those events have been transformed into strongly positive and even lighthearted remembrances.

At the same time, meaning lies hidden beneath the surface. As we saw in the last chapter, one meaning of the name "Esther" is "hidden"; and, as is often pointed out, the name of God does not appear at all in the Megillah—God's name, God's hand, is hidden behind the surface events. The sense of secret truths, of mysteries yet to be unveiled, lingers beneath all the frivolity of Chanukkah and Purim.

What are these secrets? In my view, they are the mystery of the feminine. The feminine rules over the winter in a way that expresses darkness but not foreboding—darkness as a natural part of life, like the months when many more hours are spent in the dark than in the light. This is the time of reflection, of long hours by the firelight, telling stories, of gathering together and sharing. The surface lightness of the holidays, the games and frivolity, are a way of entering this realm, especially of teaching children about the seriousness of life without frightening them. Like the kachinas of Southwest Indian tribes, they introduce children to spiritual reality in a comfortable, playful way. And this too is the feminine in action, as in the "woman of valor" passage we examined earlier: "She looks smilingly toward the future. . . . And the teaching of kindness is on her tongue."

The spiritual reality of Chanukkah and Purim is very deep. The sages taught that in the time of Mashiach, Chanukkah and Purim will continue to be celebrated while other holidays will drop away. Like the moon, whose size will increase to that of the sun, these days represent the mysteries that will then be revealed. Now we have hints, pieces of a puzzle that we can assemble only in part. For example, we have games of chance (like spinning the dreidel) that are not particularly favored in Jewish circles at other times. The letters stand for the miracle—*Nes gadol haya sham*, "A great miracle happened there"—which together with the "wheel of fortune" aspect of the game suggests again the hidden workings of God. At Purim we have costumes for changing our identity, revealing hidden dimensions of ourselves. Or, like the kachinas, we take on the masks of our ancestral spirits—Mordecai, Haman, the King, the Queen, the Jester, even the Horse—and act out a classic melodrama.[12]

At the same time, the historical stories of these times reflect the themes of courage and self-sacrifice, particularly with the heroines of the tales. We can see these as interwoven with the themes of change, renewal, hiddenness, and surprise. For surely one of the great mysteries of existence is that the willingness to sacrifice oneself, to take the risks of giving up the ego, enables one to open to one's deeper self and ultimately to God. But here we perceive it in a different way: not the serious, straight path of self-examination, repentance, atonement, nullification of the ego, with their nuances of analysis and intellect. Rather, we see the path the way a jester reveals it, or a child. The many levels of archetypes, from heroes to fools, reflect like a hall of mirrors the hidden and secret dimensions of our personal lives, the miraculous history of the Jewish people, and the mysteries of life itself.

There is a quality to Purim and its festivities, at the end of the winter season, analogous to the opening of Pandora's box, the release of the hidden creative energies that are under the rule of the feminine. Then begins again, with Pesach and springtime, the cycle of the meeting of male and female, the betrothal and marriage. Over and over again the cycle repeats itself. In our personal lives it is like a spiral: every Purim is Purim, but not the same; every Pesach, Pesach, but different. We hope to find ourselves each year on a higher rung, deepening and refining our approach to God.

This deepening happens in many ways. Simply by fuller participation in these holidays as communal events, we are bound more closely to the rhythms of Jewish life. Study of the literature about the holidays and their mitzvot also helps us develop our kavannah and bring a feminine consciousness into what we do. Most of all, the rituals and ceremonies take us on a detour from our usual analytical and practical modes of consciousness. We became actors in a play that moves at a deeper level, engaging us in a script written with the rhythm of life, the dynamics of male and female. What begins as a work of our own conscious mind, relating to Torah and tradition by adding our reflection upon it, takes us below the conscious level to the deeper meanings of our own life and to a growing love of God. The framework of ritual, thoughtfully undertaken, thus speaks to us year by year, from within our own life experience.

CHAPTER 5

Women's Mitzvot
and Feminine Reality

Channah, the mother of Shmuel the prophet, is one of the great female figures of the Bible. She is considered a powerful model for the life of prayer, as we will see below. The letters of her name, ChaNaH, are also an acronym for three mitzvot which are considered the special property of women: *challah*, *niddah*, and *hadlik ner*. Challah refers to the taking of a bit of dough from the bread one makes as a memorial of offerings to the priests in Temple times. Niddah means observing the laws of intimacy between husband and wife; and hadlik ner refers to the lighting of Shabbat candles. Two of these mitzvot, challah and lighting candles, are not unique to women; men can do them also. So what does it mean that they belong to women?

Critics have suggested that focusing on these mitzvot limits women's spiritual life to very traditional boundaries: food, sexuality, and the home.[1] But these are not the only mitzvot women are expected to do. Quite the contrary. Of the traditional number of 613 mitzvot, more than 200 are obligatory today, and most of these are an equal obligation on men and women: ritual mitzvot like keeping the holidays and Shabbat, attaching a mezuzah to one's doors, saying blessings before and after eating; ethical mitzvot like giving charity and loving one's neighbor; mitzvot of spiritual development like faith and love of God. Only a few are obligatory on men but not on women: for example, the wearing of *tzitzit* (fringes) and *tefillin* (phylacteries); prayer at set times; serving (if qualified) on a court. Custom has also elaborated some of these. The specifics of these differences in obligation are not for our present discussion. Here we need only point out that women, in common with men, have many more mitzvot than the three we are discussing here, and involvement in all of them is important to women in developing a full Jewish life.

But the "women's mitzvot" are special. Observant women often claim that these are truly the foundation of their spiritual lives. Indeed, the marks of the observant Jew today, male or female, are the observance of Shabbat, keeping kosher, and keeping "family purity"—the same areas claimed for the woman's sphere. If the areas of women's spiritual expertise are actually the foundation of Judaism as a whole, this would turn on its head the accusation that Judaism is a "patriarchal" religion.

Can these mitzvot be understood as a genuine expression of a feminine and deeply Jewish spirituality, not one externally imposed by a patriarchy trying to keep its discontented subjects in line? From my experience the answer is, very much so. While these three mitzvot do not embrace the full range of feminine expression, they are a foundation, deeply rooted in our beings, for other things that we do. One by one, let us look at them more deeply.

> *Challah, the offering of the dough,*
> *the kneading of the bread,*
> *folding and turning,*
> *the sticky lump of flour and water*
> *comes to life in the hand,*
> *springs back,*
> *lumps becoming smooth,*
> *folding and turning*
> *turning and folding,*
> *pressing,*
> *pushing,*
> *punching,*
> *there is my love,*
> *there is my anger,*
> *there is my hurried day's work,*
> *there is my relief and my joy.*
> *May blessings come to those who receive this challah.*
> *Powerful are you, God, who has made us holy,*
> *bringing the bread to rise*
> *under our hand.*
> *Here: a piece to the fire, to the offering,*
> *to the cohanim,*
> *our work, our life goes to you.*
> *We give before we eat.*

To understand the mitzvah of *challah,* we must first understand the spiritual and symbolic significance of food for women. "It is a fact cross-culturally," writes Caroline Walker Bynum, "that food is particularly a woman-controlled resource."[2] When one thinks of the number of hours women have spent preparing food—not only the regular meals but holiday feasts, special food for infants, the sick, and the elderly—cleaning up afterward, and preserving food, the thought boggles the mind. Probably more hours have been spent in women's working with food than in all the rest of our civilization building. Yet we often ignore this dimension of feminine expression, not recognizing the symbolic and traditional meanings of our cooking and eating.

Food in Judaism is rich in meaning, bringing us to the threshold of a feminine world with special qualities of its own. For example, the cooking pot is a nearly universal feminine symbol. What happens in a pot is that the inedible becomes edible, flavors intermingle, some new and unpredictable unity comes out of the diverse ingredients. This is feminine because it reflects what goes on inside our bodies. We can see this in idiomatic expressions: a visibly pregnant woman will sometimes be asked, "So you have a loaf in the oven?" Likewise, after giving birth, our bodies make milk, in the mystery and miracle of nourishment. As women we "know" these mysteries from inside ourselves. Something totally new comes from our bodies, of its own accord. This happens in a cooking pot too, at least when we are deeply involved with our cooking. As Meir Abehsera once observed,[3] elderly Moroccan women might own only one or two pots but could cook anything, naturally and effortlessly. They were masters of the pot. This is not exclusive to women, of course, but it comes from the feminine side of our natures. From outside, it is a mystery—it can even look sinister, like the lore of the witch's cauldron. But from inside, it is natural, like the growth of life or the making of milk.

The Jewish expression of the archetype of the cooking pot is—of course!—chicken soup. The clear, refined broth rich with flavors and minerals, steaming hot, is like nectar of chicken: the essence of chicken, served as a Shabbat and holiday delicacy and as a medicinal. From childhood to old age, it is the symbol of the special nourishment that the woman of the house provides. "Mama's chicken soup" should not be a joke: for women especially, food is connected with love, and especially with maternal love, just as the flowing of milk from our breasts is a response to our special relationship with our new baby. The full pot and the overflowing breast are feminine expressions of love.

Probably equal to the cooking pot as a feminine symbol is the loaf of bread—in Jewish tradition, the challah. The process of kneading and baking of bread bears some resemblance to the mysteries of the pot: an apparently stable and rather tasteless substance grows under one's hands, becomes rich with fragrance and flavor, almost as if it comes to life. In Jewish tradition bread is the staff of life. When one says a blessing over bread, that blessing covers all the other foods at the meal as well; and the thanksgiving for bread after the meal is long and filled with light, pleasant melodies. Though many women no longer make their own bread, many have renewed the tradition in recent years to make at least bread for Shabbat, and it is one of the special preparations that carries a woman's individuality.

For such special occasions as Shabbat and the holidays, we add a truly feminine touch: we braid it into what is customarily called a challah. Braiding is an archetypal feminine image, related to weaving, to the web or net. It is the act of containing energy and turning it to our own uses. As we may "do up" our hair into braids or circles, channeling the energy of our auras, or as we dance together in intricate steps and rhythms, weaving in circles, so we make elaborate chains of the springy dough. In any of these we are establishing the channels through which energy will run, anchoring it down at certain points (as in what we now refer to as "networking," which was natural to women long before it had the name). This sense of energy shaped into gracious and powerful forms is part of feminine symbolism.

As the soup pot reminds us of the inner mystery of life and the chal-lah of the weaving of energy, so also vital life energy resonates in the symbolism of the foods we serve on Jewish occasions. On Rosh Hashanah and every Shabbat we serve fish, a mild and delicate food that is a symbol of eternal life and awareness. In the fall, for Rosh Hashanah or Sukkot, we put pomegranates on the table—the fruits filled with seeds that recall nothing so much as a ripe ovary. It is said the seeds represent the 613 mitzvot (commandments): they are like seeds of spiritual light, bursting into the world from its creative source. Kreplach (traditional on Erev Yom Kippur and Hoshanah Rabbah) are said to cover our sins, but they also suggest a hidden form, like an infant grow-ing in the womb. Poppy seeds at Purim time, just before spring, are the tiny dry seeds awaiting planting, again hidden inside the cookies called hamantaschen. Pesach presents us with the impossible—a simple, flat bread as our staple food. But Jewish women have "risen" to the occa-sion, thanks to the unique frothing ability of egg whites: the result is the beloved Passover sponge cake. Then there is the custom of serving dairy on Shavuot, a tribute to the fresh products of early summer and a reminder of another kind of sensuality, if we remember Yehudit serving cheese and wine to Holofernes.

These examples simply suggest the variety of feminine life symbolism that is found in our foods. We must remember, of course, that these come from the unconscious level of our psyches; the fact that they are feminine does not automatically make any of us a good cook. But they are connected, in our minds and in traditional teaching, with the "woman of the house": with the feminine, the womb, the home, the hidden place of nurturing and growth. It is not that the woman is stuck in the kitchen but that she rules the place of nourishment and guards its spiritual quality—its kashrut—and from there rules the inner dimensions of the home. We saw with Sarah and Rivkah how their bearing of children was connected with their power and influence in family decision making: from the fruit of their womb they ruled the household. Similarly with food: the midrash tells us that their bread was always warm and fresh, reminding us that the physical nurturing that begins with a woman's body and extends to the life-giving foods she creates becomes a dimension of her influence over the whole home.

Yet because of this psychological and spiritual dimension, present in all our relations with food and heavily symbolic for women, food can become an emotional barometer of ourselves and our relationships. We see this most clearly on the negative side; for example, the outbreaks of anorexia, bulimia, and compulsive overeating in our times are evidence of the centrality of food in women's emotional lives. Kim Chernin has suggested that it is no accident that the first sin was eating—Chavah consuming the forbidden fruit of the garden—because eating is often an expression of a desire for spiritual fulfillment.[4] Certainly, women with eating disorders often testify that the emptiness of their inner life, emotionally, spiritually, or both, drives them to food as a substitute.

Food often becomes a mediator for relationships, representing nourishing and caring; even if we are not terrific cooks, we often have the impulse to cook for someone we love—and someone we love can be very hurt by our lack of interest in cooking for him. On the dark side, food can mediate destructiveness—the witch and her potions or the poison of "arsenic and old lace." Even on the nourishing side, the stereotypes tell us how women can go to extremes. We can think of the woman who sacrifices herself as victim to an abusive husband whom she loves and tries forever to please with food; or the grandmother who never listens to a word from anyone else, dominating the table with "Eat, eat!" The food itself—intended to be rich with life—can become heavy and deadening. Centuries of oppression have, I think, left us as Jews with some traditional preparations of food that are neither healthy nor gracious; as a result, Jewish cuisine is not the most admired national or ethnic food.

Nevertheless, food communicates in many healthy ways that aspect of the feminine which is giving and caring, which forms healthy bonds among people. Mother to infant and woman to her family are only the most obvious of these. A *simcha* is always accompanied by a *seudah*: when we gather together in joy, whether for a circumcision or a wedding or a Bar or Bat Mitzvah, we share a common table. Many have the custom of serving a small snack when people gather to learn, to "sweeten" our Torah study with food. The contrary—avoiding the intimate bonds that food can create—is reflected in the way Jewish law restricts the exchange between Jew and non-Jew around food. We are to eat only at a kosher table and refrain from drinking non-Jewish wine.

Besides being an expression of love and a means of bonding, food and nourishment are sensual. As nourishment comes first of all from the breast, food carries with it the sensuality of the body. The full breast, the cornucopia overflowing with delicacies, the table laden with attractive food giving off delicious aromas, the act of eating itself can be highly sensual. This sensuality can awaken our vitality. It can also go to extremes: some traditions have as a significant feminine image the cow or the sow, the earth mother heavy and dense with her own produce. It is worthy of note that rituals indulging in the eating of animals never became prominent in Judaism. Sacrifices were necessary in order for us to be allowed to eat meat, but many elements found in some other traditions—drinking the blood, indulging in the fat—were not merely disapproved but explicitly forbidden. "You shall not boil a kid in its mother's milk," the law that became our principle for separating meat and milk, guarded against another kind of idolatrous ritual. It also meant that slaughtering in order to eat was, symbolically, separated from taking nourishment from the mother, the giver of milk.

Moreover, Judaism never extended the symbolism of food to make it actually represent the spiritual, as did, for example, the Christian Eucharist. For Jews food is simply food; it is to be eaten with care and attention; it should be presented in attractive and varied form to awaken our vitality, not to overstimulate the animal appetite. We enjoy the food for the pleasure it gives us, but we take it with the ritual care and attention of priests and priestesses. Ideally our table is like the altar in the Holy Temple of ancient days: we approach it with awe and observe its rituals carefully, remembering, as we say in the grace after meals, that we are God's people.[5]

Finally, we have one remarkable custom that completely transforms the role of food in Judaism. One meal a week—the third meal of Shabbat—we are told to eat for reasons other than hunger. The spirituality of eating,

Rabbi Nachman of Breslov says, is revealed at this meal. Here one eats without hunger (having had a full meal at midday), at a time when one is in tune with one's soul after more than twenty hours of Shabbat rest and holiness. A remarkable meal it is: our refrigerator somehow still is full of food, despite having provided two full meals for family and guests. We set once more a table of delights when neither we nor anyone else is hungry. But then the beauty and richness of food stands by itself, uncomplicated by our bodily needs; so eating becomes a purely spiritual act, a mitzvah. Spiritually we are already filled. Thus, instead of accompanying our eating with a spiritual act (a blessing) to make it holy, we are accompanying our spiritual elevation with food, honoring the final moments of Shabbat with the elements of nourishment, nurture, love, and sensuality that are from the earth, from this created world.

With this spiritual awareness of food, the "woman's mitzvah" of challah takes on a far deeper dimension. The act of doing the mitzvah is quite simple: when we prepare a batch of dough, we take a piece of it—about the size of a large olive from a batch made from at least three and a half pounds of flour—as symbolic of an offering. A blessing is said, and the piece is then burned in the oven or fire. It used to be that when dough was baked for bread or matzoh, a certain proportion was given to the priests of the Temple in Jerusalem. Though the Temple no longer stands, we are still obligated to take a piece; it is burned because it cannot in these days be eaten by a priest dedicated to Temple service.

This small act puts all our nurturing, giving, bonding activities around food in a different perspective. We can give food to please others and receive compliments, we can prepare it to please ourselves, we can indulge in the smells and flavors and colors and textures of food and create a whole range of symbolism. But if we take from our bread, the staff of life, this small portion called challah, we are giving a special kind of tzedakah or charity from the heart of life. We give it, symbolically now, to nourish the work of the Temple because the Temple, as we saw in the story of Yehudit, represents the center of holiness, the womb of our spiritual life. Like the offering of first fruits and the taking of maaser (a tenth) from one's crops in the land of Israel, it is a piece of one's work that has come to life, which we now give back to the source of life. As Channah gave her son to the Temple priests, dedicating him to holy work, we dedicate our bread to the holy work of nourishing our souls as well as our bodies. The rest of the bread will be taken to our table, the extension of the Temple altar and the echo of Sarah's tent, to become the center of holy nourishment in our own families and communities.

By extension, the mitzvah of challah refers to the entire area of food: that food should be dedicated to a holy purpose and prepared in the special way described by the laws of kashrut. Further, it reminds us to be mindful of God and of God's purposes for us as women when preparing or eating food. Challah is, in effect, the center point around which revolves the entire realm of spiritual eating. And, in a profound sense—to return to the beginning—the bread itself represents us as women. The yeasted dough is the most remarkable of our formations with its aliveness and yet its malleability to the design of our hands. Dough rises and flattens, as our bodies change through puberty, pregnancy, childbirth, menopause, old age. It is said that challah is taken from the dough as the first human, Adam, was taken from the earth, and as woman was taken from the side of Adam. Other forms of tzedakah we give as a general sacrifice, reminding ourselves that all comes from God; but in taking the piece of challah, giving it to the fire, to the work of holiness, we are giving a piece of our uniquely feminine life energy, of our womanhood.

Niddah.
Can you come close?
Can I touch you?
Will you be mine?
Must I be yours?
What is this dance we play
me and you, I and thou,
far away and close, passing in the night—
how can I know you like this?
how can you know me?
how can I know me?
Together and apart
we become something new
a new possibility in creation.

Many regard the rituals of *taharat hamishpocheh,* "family purity," as obsolete today. Yet we find more and more young women taking them on. What leads women to choose a practice that involves sexual abstinence part of the time? More generally, what are we to make of a system that gives women no choice about the expression of their sexuality? The halacha stipulates that for our entire menstrual period plus seven more days each month we must practice abstinence from sexual relations. So, of course, must our husbands, who also have no choice. (They have a less direct relation to the system, since it is the woman's biology that dictates the times of separation and union.)

Should we be coerced by our biology at all, though? Although we are women and our breasts give milk, although because we resonate to symbols of food and nourishment, we do not necessarily become chief cook and table setter in the household. Why then, because of our periods, must we follow a sexual schedule? Is this some scheme to make sure we have more babies?

It is tempting to turn to the interesting studies that have been conducted in the past several years on the differences women experience in their feelings, inclinations, and abilities at different times in their menstrual cycle. For example, some have argued that there are rhythms in most women's lives that are represented by the poles of ovulation and menstruation. The time of menstruation is characterized by withdrawal and inwardness, often accompanied by vivid dreams; the pole of ovulation is marked by outgoingness and greater openness to socializing. Recent Canadian research in women's cognitive ability indicates that women operate more skillfully in different areas according to their low or high estrogen levels, verbal and fine motor skills being at their peak when estrogen is high (ovulation), spatial skills when it is low (menstruation). Claims have been made (and disputed) that the chemistry of our bodies is such that it is actually healthier to avoid sex during and immediately after menstruation.

But none of the extant studies is definitive; and none can really tell us how we should act when menstruating or ovulating, only what variations and consequences we can expect when we undertake certain kinds of activity. We are not like animals whose sexual activity is restricted to certain times: we can do almost anything from sex to mathematics at any time we please, and most of us suffer no ill effects.

Still, we may find that we are more in harmony with our own nature if we follow the rhythms in our bodies. These bodily changes, however, are subtle. Beyond physical symptoms and a heightened emotionality or irritability at certain times, many of us are not very much aware of how our personal moon phase, so to speak, affects what we are doing and how we are relating. Even if we are aware, we are taught to hide or belittle the differences. Tribal and ancient cultures set up a variety of rituals of seclusion for women, but in the modern West culture has killed our sensitivity to nature.

As a result, we have arrived at the point where we can be expected to perform on a nine-to-five, fifty-week-a-year job, or cook and keep house equally well every week for our families, or accomplish our multitudinous tasks with equal efficiency every day. We might be forgiven for some oversights during "that time of the month," but these are considered weaknesses rather than signs that we might do better directing our energy in another path. These attitudes reveal that despite our intentions to be positive, open, and honest about our physiology our culture is still intolerant of menstruation. We no longer view the menstruating woman as actually dangerous, one who pollutes all she touches and who must be segregated. But we have no positive vision of this time. Our culture has offered instead the sexless, or at least hormoneless, woman: she who never falters or shows extremes no matter what her body is doing.

Jewish tradition suggests a different path, neither the tribal way of radical seclusion nor modern culture's path of ignoring feminine rhythms. The Torah defines precisely what is at issue. Variable moods, inclinations, or abilities are only the superficial symptoms of something much deeper. Even the obvious physical purposes of ovulation and menstruation— repeatedly preparing the body for pregnancy—are really on the surface. The entire process is something else: a scale drawing, so to speak, of the creativity of the universe.

The pivotal point of that creativity is the union of male and female. As we saw earlier, this is manifest ritually in the movement of Shabbat and the cycle of the year. The female rhythms lay the foundation, the male brings forth the spark. On the human level, her rhythms are decisive: there is a time for union and a time for separation. While the descriptions of the time of *niddah* are usually translated "impurity" or "uncleanness," they do not connote magical danger or pollution, let alone dirt. The time is viewed negatively only from the point of view that now creative union cannot properly take place. No other pollution is involved, no other relationships are forbidden. The only things not permitted at this time are entering into sexual relations, and gestures between husband and wife that might lead to such relations.

There are many implications of following these rhythms. The separation for nearly two weeks alters the relationship between husband and wife. Many of us know, from the times we suffer discomfort from our periods, that we want warmth and caring without sexual demands. If we are not suffering, we do not notice this need so sharply. But many observant women report that their relationships are enriched by the cycle precisely because of the shift to another style of relationship between husband and wife. "It's not just on the physical level," many say. Caring takes place in a different way. As when a woman feels too ill to cook, her continual loving-through-nourishment shifts into another gear, so when she becomes more inward or needy, her husband must transform his sexual loving into another form.

For us apart from our partners there are other benefits. At the time of
niddah a woman does not come near her husband. This is our solitude,
our darkness, our hiddeness—an opportunity to go inward, that can lead
to a spiritual focus. When we take additional time out for spiritual pursuits during the days of niddah, it can sometimes relieve emotional
distress—the anxiety, deflated energy, or depression that many of us
experience at this time. Some women find it a fortuitous time for dreams
or visualizations that give us insight or comfort.

The time of niddah is also a time of preparation. After finding our
place of solitude, we move into the other rhythm, preparing to join again
with our husbands. Jewish mysticism tells us that when husband and
wife unite at permitted times, and especially on Shabbat or at the end of
her period of niddah when it is a mitzvah to do so, their union reflects the
union of masculine and feminine in the divine. This is a special kind of
holy act: two people in their physical being and their natural energies
reflect the culmination of the divine creative process, making a unity
from what had been a duality. The two who had been separated, like
Adam and Chava, now come together as God and the world.

This is the essential reason why Jews do not practice celibacy. Marriage is important—so important that the blessing on a newborn infant is
that he or she will be raised to "Torah, chupah [marriage], and good
deeds." More than in any other tradition, marriage is of the essence of
Jewish work in the world. Only in the union between man and woman
can we touch with our own natures the process that the whole world is
about: to come together, to overcome our separation, to be at one. At-
one-ness in Judaism comes in an act of pleasure and creativity, as though
God made the world just for this.

In these rituals we can also hear the echo, in our own practice, of the
holiness discussed in chapter 2: sexuality is to be guarded, preserved for
the right times, as a powerful source of creativity. In marriage we develop
the discipline that makes this possible. Romantic love is egotistical, seeking one round after another of pleasurable feelings, but with no further aim.
Even extended "relationships" that go beyond mere romance are founded
primarily on the desires of the partners for companionship and security—
essentially self-centered aims. As Jewish women, as sexual beings, we aim
at holiness, so our partnership is different, beginning with the sexual
dimension. It is essential to set apart the time and place. We count the days,
prepare ourselves for the monthly renewal that comes with immersion in
a mikvah. Together with our husbands, we develop the discipline of abstinence and careful attention to the nature of our contact and speech.

Then our monthly immersion is truly an experience of renewal. Water, especially the gathering of waters in a pool, is part of a nearly universal feminine symbolism.[6] "Mikvah" means the gathering of waters, and immersion is always in either a natural body such as a pond or sea or an indoor pool specially constructed so as to be connected to naturally gathered waters, like a pool of fresh rainwater. The waters of a mikvah are, as Rabbi Aryeh Kaplan pointed out, connected to the waters of Eden,[7] the original rivers that flowed from the garden. They make for us each month a rebirth of spiritual virginity.

The rhythm of this "woman's mitzvah" highlights a different dimension of her experience of herself in relationship—not this time through nourishing and nurturing, but through the dynamic of withdrawal and joining, separation and union. We move from inwardness to transformation and renewal, then to the willingness to give ourselves to another in a coming together that mirrors the union of the world with its source. Individuality and independence are balanced at a deep level with interdependence and mutual surrender. The rites and practices make for a demanding path in some ways, while in other respects nothing could seem more natural. The practices of *taharat hamishpocheh* ensure that the structure of intimacy in a family is founded on the woman's inner rhythms, an anchor to the inner psychic life of the family and the people, a ground of holiness in our relationships.

Hadlik Ner.
The house is prepared.
Orderly, awaiting the guests—
Somehow it never manages to look this clean on weekdays.
Suddenly a moment of silence
the universe is hushed, waiting
she raises her hands
making three circles
bringing forth the world of holiness
here into this world,
into this house, this room
where we will truly live
and never forget
and never want to leave.

Shabbat is the great miracle of Jewish life. How is it that the house feels so different, that food never tastes so good? And how is it that this is so intimately connected with women? Men can certainly light Shabbat candles, and should if no woman is there to do it. They are obligated equally with women to "remember Shabbat and keep it holy." Although we have seen that Shabbat has long been mystically associated with feminine energy, it would be circular to argue that this proves it should be a woman's mitzvah. Besides, if men call forth Shabbat, so to speak, in Friday evening's davening, why should there be a different and special mitzvah at home?

Part of the connection is that Shabbat is directly related to the home. Shabbat begins at home first, and ends there with *havdalah*. But this does not explain everything, unless we resort to the cliché that woman's place is in the home. A clean house and a refrigerator full of food does not make Shabbat. So we cannot do without a deeper understanding of the connection among woman, home, and Shabbat.

We have spoken thus far about two "mysteries" associated with women: the creation of nourishment from our bodies and our moonlike rhythms that not only prepare us for pregnancy but also allow us to develop the dynamics of a mature relationship. There is a third mystery, the most inward of all: the interior orientation of women's spirituality. Women often find it natural to describe spirituality and the divine in inward terms. The prophetess in the cave, Sarah in her tent, Rivkah and Rachel by the wells, the universal symbolism of spiritual seeking in pools of water or in darkness suggest that inwardness. Not that a woman cannot appear in public or do public things, but she need not seek outward for spirituality; the treasure is the inner self. The fact that men sometimes take this literally, as meaning a woman should stay at home, may mean they see the woman as a symbol for their own security: she is a place for him to go, and an assurance of his own inwardness.

Inwardness is best sought in privacy, a protected space, not in the public domain where many feet trample and many people's paths cross at random. This is true in most spiritual traditions. The monk has a cell; the prophet a cave or a tent; the sage a study.[8] Even those who go for spiritual refreshment out of doors seek the quiet, undisturbed spaces in nature.

For Judaism the home—not the cell of the celibate—is the epitome of the private place. Woman is connected with interiority, inwardness, and so with the private space of the home. Shabbat too is connected with the movement inward, with privacy and intimacy, rather than the busyness of the outside world. Abraham Heschel has cited Rabbi Shimeon bar Yochai as saying that "all mitzvot, all commandments, the Holy One gave to Israel in public, except the Sabbath which was given in privacy, 'between Me and Israel.'"[9] The mystery of Shabbat is, as we saw above, the mystery of the union of the Y-H-V-H, the masculine, transcendent aspect of God, with the Shekhinah, the feminine, immanent aspect of God. Reflected in the union of husband and wife on Shabbat, it is the ultimate joy of Shabbat itself. For the man, this is symbolized in his making Kiddush, for the cup of wine represents the feminine.[10] This is his part in bringing together what is separate: husband and wife, male and female, God and the world—a movement inward, proclaiming a toast to home and to the place of the feminine.

The feminine, then, is deeply connected to Shabbat, and it is natural that women should have a crucial role creating the day. But what of the lighting of candles? This mitzva of Shabbat is not mentioned anywhere in the Torah itself, but lighting candles on Friday night is probably one of the most widely known mitzvot of Judaism. The midrash says that Sarah, long before the Torah was given, lit candles. Perhaps it was a voluntary custom among Jewish women from time immemorial.

The meaning of this light comes through in two images, in striking parallel, from the midrash. One is the story that before a child is born, an angel comes to the child in the womb, lights a candle, and learns Torah with the unborn infant. The second is that on Shabbat angels come to the home to see if the candles are lit and the house is prepared, and they give a favorable blessing if all is well. In both examples the place of growth and blessing, the place that attracts spiritual energy (the angels), is feminine space, the womb and the interior of the home. Similarly, a recurring image in women's spirituality is the cave lit by a fire. When light illuminates the space of darkness, a new spiritual potential appears, not yet formed and articulate in the world. When a woman lights Shabbat candles, she affirms her power to create holy time and space according to her inner light, the light of her soul in its connection to God, her most deeply felt sense of goodness, plenitude, and peace. Like the womb inside, without which no child can grow, the Shabbat lights create an interior without which spirituality cannot enter the world.

Thus the Shabbat candles remind us also of the lights of creation. As the first thing God spoke was, "Let there be light," so we celebrate the culmination of creation with the lighting of lights. That first light created by God had a special quality, so that, the midrash says, one could see from one end of the world to the other. It was so powerful that God put it away, to be revealed again to the righteous at the end of days. Shabbat light is like that light, just as Shabbat itself is like the world to come. Rabbi Chaim of Krasne saw Shabbat as the well from which the life of paradise takes its source—the well, the mysterious inner depths. Something of eternity comes into our souls with the Shabbos lights, something of that ability to know, to see forever.[11] These depths of knowledge are connected with the interiority of feminine spirituality.

In today's world of spirituality we tend to look for inspiration to charismatic leaders or at least polished orators. We judge institutions by their social impact: how many people are attracted to this, or what good causes are supported here—support for refugees, work in the peace movement, or discussions of current issues. The quiet work that we do to bring in Shabbat is largely ignored. We will acknowledge that being together on Friday night is good for the family, but we can't imagine anything else.

But here we are reminded again of the "hiddenness" of Esther. In truth, nothing else can take place without this space that is protected from the incursions of the outside: no birth without a womb, no redemption without Shabbat. Unless we provide the space of preparation, the place for the unformed potential, nothing new can come into being. Thus we must have Shabbat, for the sake of the world. We must create space that is empty—empty of work, of our creative activity, of material affairs. We must light that space with the spiritual power and insight of the feminine, and all the capacities that implies. Then we can help give birth in the next week to a new world; then the world can be infused with the values of Shabbat: devotion to godliness, striving for holiness, plenitude, and peace.

It is said that Sarah's candles stayed lit from one Shabbat to the next—just as the Temple had a *ner tamid*, a "continuous light." The special power of her Shabbat, to bring light and joy and unity into the world, did not end on Shabbat itself. From her tent and likewise from the Temple, blessings continued to fill the world. This is indeed within our power, when we make Shabbat lights and Shabbat unity part of our spiritual consciousness. In the next chapter we will look more closely at how we can develop that power in our inner lives.

CHAPTER 6

Inner Voices

Looking for God:
Blessed is the glory of the Lord from his place!
And where is the place of his glory?
Looking inward,
between the words,
in the silence,
in the song,
in the letters,
in the space that opens for us—
where is the place of his glory?

We can experience a great deal of satisfaction, even exhilaration, as we learn to tune our minds and hearts to the rhythms of natural cycles and spiritual dimensions of existence: our biological rhythms, the seasons, and the history of divine action in the world. As we enrich our lives with ritual, we find ourselves more deeply connected to Jewish community and more deeply affected by the wisdom that comes from our tradition. Yet we yearn for something more—an inward connection with God that brings us serenity in the midst of our busy lives, a knowledge that God speaks to us and guides us, and a comfort that we can speak to God.

Sometimes this closeness happens easily and naturally, and we wonder why we do not have it all the time. We seem to live much of the time with a shell around our soul, a barrier to God. While sometimes it seems an opening appears in the shell of its own accord, most of time it seals up again and has to be broken through again and again. This is the difficult work of developing a spiritual life.

We spoke earlier of how certain rituals are particularly effective in changing one's state of consciousness, opening a person to other levels of receptivity, moving toward the "prophetic" end of the spectrum. All religious traditions have methods for doing this. Prayer, meditation, discipline of the body, music and rhythm—all these have been used by spiritual seekers throughout the ages. Such practices tend to show less gender preference, presumably because they are more inward oriented. They have not so much to do with how we express ourselves in knowing, shaping, and responding to the world as with our inner core, which, most mystics attest, is a more nearly androgynous level of being. While those with the leisure to pursue mystical consciousness have more often been men, and some have tried to keep women away, women who have entered upon these paths have usually found the techniques just as accessible and useful to them as to men.

It is also true that in describing our experiences, vocabulary and metaphors may sometimes be gender specific. For example, male descriptions of spiritual experience often speak of moving up and out, while female metaphors point down and in. Caroline Bynum's study of medieval women found the metaphors of feast and fast much more central to their descriptions than to men's. But in the actual practice of prayer or meditation there are not always clear distinctions. Thus, many of the things I will speak of in this chapter are not specific to women alone. Still, it is important that women find the voice to speak of what happens when we move away from the everyday level of experience of self, and beyond the concreteness of ritual, to something that we recognize as the divine, as God, inside and outside the self.

How in Judaism do we make this move? We must postpone a direct answer to this question until we set the stage. Every tradition provides a context for the spiritual search, a foundation—a person's age, experience, soundness of character, ability to accept discipline and follow a steady course. In short, we must accept the requirements of a sound life, maintaining this side-by-side with any explorations we wish to make in personal spirituality. Living a consciously Jewish life in our homes and communities, celebrating the holidays and practicing Jewish rituals, intensifies our yearning and our seriousness of intent. We commit ourselves to the life of mitzvot—even if we are not ready to observe all of them to the same degree. It is taught that when we say the first paragraph of the Shema, we take on the "yoke of heaven," accepting the idea that

God guides the world and is our guide. In saying the second paragraph, we take on the "yoke of the commandments." We accept, in other words, the necessity of spiritual discipline.

Yet the mitzvot are not merely a set of rules but a system to bring one to God. We can speak of the taking on of the "yoke" as consenting to having our consciousness opened; then the doing of mitzvot actually is the cultivation of that consciousness—like plowing and fertilizing a field—for higher levels of contact with the divine. Every religious act in Judaism aims at a connection with God and cumulatively has the effect of sensitizing a person to the work of God in the world.

This happens in two ways. First, with every mitzvah consciously performed, we adopt the general intention, of which we spoke in chapter 4, of doing what God wants of us. Our action becomes an extension of the divine will—our hand writing a check for charity becoming an extension of God's "hand," our feet walking to synagogue becoming God's "feet," our mouths speaking kindly God's "mouth."

Second, as we bring more of a Jewish rhythm and order to our lives, we are changed: we become more sensitive to our environment, more aware of harmony and discord, more "observant" in the ordinary sense of the term. As a Mormon acquaintance once put it, quite succinctly, "Order brings discernment." As Jews we become sensitive to elements in our lives that we never noticed before. When we begin paying attention to *kashrut* we discover all kinds of things about products sold in the stores that we never knew—and are sometimes shocked to learn. When we live in tune with the Jewish day, week, and year we become more aware of sunrise, sunset, the phases of the moon. As we take on the discipline of tithing (giving a tenth) to charity, we become more aware of the power of money in our lives, and we begin to study the relationships that are created with money. Every practice creates an opening for learning, making clearer distinctions, becoming more careful about how we walk in the world, and each mitzvah involves endless levels of learning. Gradually we learn to contribute to the world in more delicate, understanding ways; and we learn how the world influences us for good or ill.

Some of this learning comes simply as a by-product of practice. Just as when we clean a room, we suddenly start seeing all the other things that need to be done, so when we "clean house" with the mitzvot of Judaism, we find, perhaps to our surprise, new light shining on different corners of our world. In addition, however, we learn in a direct and conscious way, for one of the great mitzvot of Judaism is to study Torah itself. This is so important, for modern women especially, that we must look at it in some depth.

Torah study, the sages said, is the equivalent of all the other mitzvot—and it has been discussed at length how this is so. By "Torah" we do not mean just the five books of Moses, the *Chumash* ("Five"), but all the literature of commentary, law, and interpretation that are used in traditional Judaism to understand the meaning of the Five Books. The emphasis on study and understanding of this literature is a feature of spiritual practice unique to Judaism. While other traditions certainly have their sacred texts, the study of them is often optional or reserved for the few. In Judaism the opposite has always been true. Even young children learn that at Mount Sinai the Jewish people, when offered the Torah, responded, "*Naaseh v'nishmah,*" "We will do" and "We will hear." First we do the acts, then we "hear," that is, we work at understanding them more and more deeply.

In generation after generation this has meant a strong emphasis on study. Just as American values insisted on universal literacy in order to produce good citizens, so Judaism has insisted on universal Torah study in order to produce good Jews. It is true that in the past women's obligations to learn Torah were regarded by the general public and by some rabbis as minimal. We were supposed to learn just enough to practice correctly. Even if that had been the only standard, it was more than was expected of women in many non-Jewish settings. But even in ancient times there were many who upheld learning for women, so long as the setting for learning was separate from men. In modern times more and more religious leaders have been promoting serious Torah education for women.[1]

Many orthodox rabbis now would agree that women's responsibility includes learning halacha pertaining to all the mitzvot to which we are obligated, that is, all the negative and most of the positive ones (excluding some of those that are time-bound); and studying the range of literature pertaining to faith, devotion, love and fear of God—those mitzvot having to do with thought rather than action. This would include midrash, aggadah, musar, and, if one is inclined, Chassidus or kabbalah. Chumash (the Five Books of Torah) and Tanach (the Bible) are of course included, as the foundation for these others.[2] Our obligations do not inlude talmudic literature that ranges outside practical halacha and religious faith—primarily, the abstract discussions of derivations of the laws. However, there is nothing to prevent women from studying more than we are obligated, if this enriches our Jewish life and practice.[3]

Torah study affects us on many levels. It adds important dimensions to one's ritual, ethical, and spiritual practice. By studying we develop a sense for the interrelatedness of what we are doing and why, the connection of each practice to all the others. We learn to develop our *kavannah*, our intention, to engage our whole selves in our practice. But in addition, rather unexpectedly, studying Torah can break through the shell of the soul, making us more receptive to the divine. This is a great discovery of the Jewish tradition: that study can become a mystical experience. It is in this respect that Torah study is equal to all the rest of the mitzvot. In his book *The Long Shorter Way*, Rabbi Adin Steinsaltz writes that "when a person is engaged in Torah without ulterior motive, he may be said to be united with the Divine Will. He is thinking God's thoughts concerning God's world. . . . The one who is engaged in Torah becomes a part of the Shechinah itself . . . far beyond anything that is of the world."[4] This is a remarkable statement: we hardly ever think of the act of reading, learning, or repeating words in a book as an experience that can unite us with God. But Torah study is different, as many can attest who have compared it with ordinary reading or academic studies. If the mitzvot cultivate our minds, Torah plants the seeds that connect us directly to the Source of our life.

All Torah (including the centuries of commentary) partakes of the original revelation from God to Moses, then to the other prophets, and on down through the special transmission of tradition to the sages who followed. Torah is, in short, a work of *Ruach HaKodesh*, the Holy Spirit. It comes from the prophetic end of the spectrum of religious experience and unites with the intellect as it comes through the words of the sages. Moreover, Torah involves much more than anything it refers to in the world, such as history or specific legal ruling. Every word and letter carries a meaning, apart from the story or law in which it appears. Torah is like a great reservoir of God's thoughts, expanding in all directions. We might say that Torah is something like the collective unconscious of the Jewish people, the thoughts of the collective divine soul that God created for us. The sentences, words, and letters of the texts we study are our entry point into that soul level—as, by analogy, dreams and images may be an entry point into our personal unconscious. Thus, studying Torah is an opening to many dimensions of our own soul in connection with God.

As a spiritual practice, Torah study is different from prayer or meditation or the kavannah we attach to our rituals. In these other modes we are the agents, the creators of our mode of communion with God; in study of Torah we are the receivers. Our kavannah in other activities can vary according to our mood, our will, our decisions as to when, how, and what to do. Torah has a certain objectivity about it. It is what it is. At other times we set out to create a meeting with God on our own terms; Torah study is on God's terms. Although one can develop one's own personal interpretations, and one may have certain feelings or responses to a passage, these are after the fact and do not alter the basic experience: the text is there and we confront it. That soul confrontation might be awesome or surprising, or it may not have any conscious manifestation at all, remaining hidden to bear fruit much later. Nevertheless, the meeting between God and the soul takes place whenever one engages in the study of Torah.

Torah and mitzvot, then, should not be viewed simply as standard and perhaps burdensome features of traditional Jewish life. They have effects on the individual who practices and studies that go far beyond what one could imagine from looking at them from the outside. And, in this connection, I want to mention also one particularly relevant subcategory of Torah study that directly involves self-development: the spiritual house cleaning that opens us to greater spiritual receptivity. (For present purposes I am distinguishing this aspect of study from learning the how-to's of ritual practice or the contents of a biblical book.)

This part of Torah is what is usually called ethics. In the secular culture it is assumed that everyone knows basic ethical behavior: treating people kindly, not stealing or killing. There are just a few gray areas (say, sexual behavior) created by the changes of the modern world. And of course there are things that nearly everyone finds difficult to do, such as not lying, gossiping, or cheating. But ethics is assumed to be universally applicable, highly relative to situations, and fairly easy to understand.

Most spiritual traditions recognize, however, a higher level of ethical consciousness than the ordinary. When we enter on the Jewish path of self-development, we find an extraordinary quality of approach to ethics. While ethical principles may be generally known, thanks to the diffusion of the Bible throughout Western culture, their application, their reasons, and their implications in our daily lives are generally not known. For example, a class of mine began to study the category of prohibitions known as *loshon hara*, the "evil tongue." These stem from the commandment, "you shall not be a talebearer among your people," but many more biblical commandments are also involved. As we learned the details of situations in which one cannot speak about others or listen to derogatory remarks, our amazement grew. We found we had to work on changing the character of most of our casual, everyday speech. This in turn made us aware of the resentments we carry and want to express, the inordinate desires we have to hear "juicy gossip," and in general of the negative feelings—bitterness, anxiety, arrogance—that we carry with us all the time.

In short, what we found was that the study of an ethical practice in Judaism was not merely a matter of arguing over when a rule applies to a situation. It led deeper into examining our behavior and the feelings and desires underlying our actions. This in turn helped clear up other aspects of our lives for a better relationship to God. As psychotherapy can unblock our resistance to good relationships or deprogram our standard reactions to situations, so the study of Torah ethics can lead us to self-examination and personal transformation that opens us more and more.

For in Judaism one does not develop much inward depth without working on one's outward behavior, without examining, correcting, doing what is called *tshuvah* ("turning" or "return"). There is a continual dialectic between the inner and the outer: one moves from prayer to working on a personal relationship, to preparing for Shabbat, to political work, to study, to observing and correcting one's actions, and back again. The sages tell us that tshuvah was created before the world: the possibility of return, of turning around, had to be there from the beginning. Human beings, as imperfect creatures, are bound to make mistakes. And, because we have egos, we often deny that our mistakes were mistakes, and we go on digging ourselves deeper into them. The layers and layers of the negative results of our actions could be impossible to overcome if not for tshuvah.

Moreover, tshuvah is a work for everyone, not just sinners: it also means returning to God in a more complete way. Each day, as Rabbi Nachman of Breslov said, we can be doing tshuvah for the previous day, reaching for a higher level. And when we reach the next level, we see that what we did before was much less than we now can do. Thus the great *tzaddikim*, the righteous ones, took an accounting of their lives not just before Yom Kippur, but the day before each New Moon ("Yom Kippur Katan," a little Yom Kippur); and not just then, but every Friday before Shabbat; and even every day. This checking in with ourselves — reviewing what our feelings were, our actions, how we were in tune or out of tune with the world around us, how we helped or hurt others, how we helped or hurt ourselves — is part of developing a stronger foundation in our spiritual lives.

With this foundation we can begin to speak of personal spiritual work. In Jewish tradition this takes many forms, but the primary means of developing a rich relationship to God has been through prayer, and specifically the prayers set forth in the Siddur. At first this may seem strange: we usually think of the deeper opening of the soul as progressing by moving away from words, away from the conscious, verbal shaping of the world; but prayer is intensely verbal. Nevertheless, the aim is the same. In prayer we do not leave words entirely behind, but we move into a different mode of using them.[5] We can see this from the model that the sages of the Talmud recommended for prayer. For both men and women the exemplary prayer is that of a woman, namely, Channah, the mother of Shmuel HaNavi (Samuel the Prophet).

Channah's story is told at the very beginning of the book of Shmuel (1 Sam. 1:1–2:10). As we mentioned briefly above, Channah was childless, while her co-wife, Pnina, had a number of children. Although her husband, Elkanah, favored her and gave her a double portion from all his sacrifices, she was not happy, and Pnina constantly taunted her. Her distress was so great that when they went on their yearly pilgrimage to the temple at Shiloh (this was before the Temple in Jerusalem existed), Channah simply wept and could not eat. "Am I not more to you than ten sons?" Elkanah asked. But his love did not comfort her.

After the feast she went to the temple and cried inwardly, vowing to God that if he would give her a son, "then I will give him to God all the days of his life, and a razor will never touch his head." Eli the priest, who was sitting near the temple door, saw her lips moving but heard no voice, so he thought she was drunk. When he reprimanded her, she explained her grief and anxiety; he blessed her that her prayer should be granted.

Channah did indeed bear a child, Shmuel, and after he was weaned (probably at the age of three or four) took him to Eli along with a sacrifice, explaining that this was the child for whom she had prayed and that he would now be dedicated to the service of God. Shmuel went on to become a great judge and *navi* (prophet) who led Israel for many years and anointed Israel's first two kings.

Channah is regarded as the model of prayer because of the quality of her inward prayer, the prayer where her lips moved but no voice sounded, where she looked like a drunken woman. Channah was in a state of being where, we might say, the prayer prayed itself. Self-consciousness gone, her soul spoke effortlessly to God. This intensity and inwardness was what our sages admired and urged us to seek in our relationship to God.

Yet when we begin to pray, we find a paradox: we often experience our attempts simply to pray spontaneously as becoming more self-conscious rather than less. This is probably why, through the ages, the recommended approach is to take on the discipline of praying from the Siddur, our basic collection of established prayers that has been compiled from experience, from centuries of efforts to come near to God. As a result, its contents have awakened the Jewish spirit, over and over again, down to the present day.

The prayer services, and particularly Shacharit, the morning service and major prayer of the day, offer us a kind of map of human spirituality.

Davening within this pattern provides keys to unlock the shells around our souls. Often the parts of the service are described as a kind of ladder to God. Another metaphor, which I prefer, is to think of them as rooms that open up, one into another, leading to a richer and more intense experience until the soul is truly open to God. We will look briefly at some pieces from the service to orient us in understanding our own inner work.

The principal parts of the service are the morning blessings, the verses of praise (Pesuke, d'Zima), the Shema and its blessings, and the Eighteen Blessings (Shemoneh Esreh), also known as the Amidah or standing prayer.[6] The first room we enter, the morning blessings, is a series of thanks to God for our life and our personal physical existence, for his continual care of us in providing for our basic needs and making us who we are:

> Blessed are you, Lord our God, Ruler of the Universe,
> who formed humans with wisdom. You placed within us
> ducts and tubes in the shape of your glory. . . .
> My God, you gave me my soul, it is pure; you created
> it, you formed it, you placed it within me . . . you
> will take it from me. . . . At every moment my soul is
> within me, I give thanks to you. . . .
> Blessed are you, Lord our God, Ruler of the Universe,
> who gave us the ability to tell day from night . . .
> who opens our eyes . . .
> who frees the captives . . .
> who straightens the bowed . . .
> who clothes the naked . . .
> who strengthens the weary . . .
> who spreads the earth above the waters. . . .

Each blessing reminds us of a different aspect of our being and in a sense awakens each part of us to the new morning and the new day ahead. Our parts and levels, so to speak, become connected spiritually as well as physically when we acknowledge their source.

The second room contains psalms and other biblical "verses of praise," which praise God's work in all of existence. Here we express our awareness of the life of the universe of which we are a part and on which we depend, and our consciousness that this too comes from God. The Pesuke d'Zimra are a kind of mandala in words. They evoke in our imagination the entirety of creation, in motion around us, each part singing its own songs of praise to the Creator, which we echo in our being. For example:

Praise the Lord. Praise the Lord from the heavens; praise him in the celestial heights. Praise him, all his angels; praise him, all his hosts. Praise him, sun and moon; praise Him, all the shining stars, . . . heaven of heavens, and the waters above the heavens. . . . Praise the Lord from the earth, sea monsters and all that dwell in the depths; fire and hail, snow and vapor, stormy wind carrying out his command; mountains and all hills, fruit-bearing trees and all cedars; the beast and all cattle, creeping things and winged fowl; kings of the earth and all nations, rulers and all judges of the land; young men and maidens, elders together with young lads. Let them praise the Name of the Lord! (Psalm 148)

In singing the Pesuke d'Zimra we see a panorama of God's creation and his acts in history, and we enter into it with our own praise. Many of the songs also are considered to have mystical significance, using repetitions of God's names, referring to the divine attributes, or using an alphabetical structure to represent the creative work of God. The effect of the Verses of Song is to widen one's perspective to all creation, to connect with the divine forces of the universe in relation to God.

The next section, the Shema and its blessings, evokes deeper mysteries of the universe. In the first blessing we affirm God as creator of the "lights," the luminaries that are channels for the life force in our world; and we assert that God renews the creation each day, each moment. We hear the various levels of angels praising God: *Kadosh, kadosh, kadosh, Adonai tzvaot!* "Holy, holy, holy is the Lord of hosts!" and *Baruch k'vod Adonai mimkomo!* "Blessed is the glory of the Lord from his place!" The mystical affirmations of the angels usher us into unknown realms, beyond the creation where we usually feel at home. Here we feel somewhat at sea with the unfamiliar references to angels and other holy creatures. Study of Chassidus or Kabbalah can bring at least some of the angelic discourse within our range, until we begin to feel more comfortable with these elements of prayer. In any case, we can become more aware how the prayer service works with our minds, to deepen and expand our consciousness of the created universe.

The second blessing follows, thanking God for his love for us:

Lord our God, you have loved us with everlasting love. . . . *Avinu malkenu,* for the sake of our forebears who trusted in you, and whom you taught the laws that bring eternal life, to carry out your will with a perfect heart, be gracious to us and teach us. . . . Enlighten our eyes in your Torah, make our hearts cleave to your *mitzvot,* and unite our hearts to love and fear your Name. . . . You are God who

performs acts of deliverance, and you have chosen us from all nations and tongues and have brought us near to your great Name . . . that we may praise you and proclaim your Oneness and love your Name. Blessed are you who chooses his people Israel with love.

The placement of this blessing here tells us something important. God's choosing of the Jewish people with compassion, the divine love for us, expresses as great a mystery in the universe as the existence of spiritual beings, higher forces, and other worlds. We ask that we be given understanding and discernment, to know how to live in the light of this love, and that our hearts will love in response. We are here, now, at a level where our awe at God's creation turns personal and emotional. Then we say the Shema, affirming the divine unity and our willingness to learn to love God in return:

> Hear, O Israel, the Lord is our God, the Lord is One.
> Blessed be the name of the glory of his kingdom forever.
> You shall love the Lord your God with all your heart,
> with all your soul, and with all your strength. . . .

We express our awareness of our distinctive, unique relationship to God, which goes beyond being part of nature. The section closes with an affirmation of the great redemptive power of God—the miracles he has done in the past, especially bringing the Israelites out of Egypt. This ultimate expression of love and compassion is in Judaism the model for understanding God to the extent that is humanly possible. We unite with the Hebrew ex-slaves in expressing our wonder and awe: "Who is like you, Lord, among the supernal beings? Who is like you, resplendent in holiness, awesome in praise, performing wonders! . . . The Lord shall reign forever and ever!"

Awe, mystery, and love combine to bring us—if we have been able to follow the path so far this day—to the fourth room. Here we can approach God in the most intimate way: the silent prayer of the Amidah when, like Channah, our lips move but we can barely hear our own voices. This is the *tefillah* (*the* prayer) in its essence. Composed of a series of petitions combined with blessings acknowledging God's power, they convey many—sometimes all—of the things for which we might wish to ask God; and we add our own personal petitions as well. This is the level of prayer praying itself, and the words are to express the deep, nearly universal wishes for our life in the world. Yet the words are to go beyond the words, to be in a state of awareness such that the words are merely a channel to give some form to one's connection with God. We may experi-

ence deep emotion, or we may reach into silence. And it may take many years of prayer before the Amidah, the standing before God, means anything at all.

To become familiar with the Siddur, with the words and phrases that have been cherished by the Jewish people for centuries, is a work of love. Its map of humanity's approach to the divine, from the physical world to the deeply mystical, to the personal and inward, reminds us of the turn we must make in our lives to grow closer to God. Each prayer or psalm can become an inspiration for deeper thought, a reassurance for faith, and a reservoir of strength in times of difficulty. Yet for some, that familiarity may be hard to come by, particularly if one's ability to read Hebrew is weak. English translations, even when they do reasonable justice to the Hebrew, often sound stilted and formal. While almost anyone who has worked at learning Hebrew as a language of prayer will attest that the results are well worth the effort, still we often need additional resources.

In addition, many women have objections to the masculine references to God, or to the hierarchical tone of the descriptions—God as King, Judge, and so on. Of course, God is beyond gender and beyond any particular descriptions; the phrases we have at hand were meant only to convey some experience of God—of strength, of mercy, of justice—that can enrich our understanding and hence our relationship to God. But the words, English or Hebrew, do not always work for us as well as they could.

Besides, devout people have long recognized that the prayers of the Siddur alone may not always awaken the depths we need to reach in ourselves. There is a line at the beginning of Ashrei, "Happy are those who dwell in your house, they will praise you forever." *Yoshvei*, usually translated "those who dwell," can also mean "those who sit"; thus one interpretation of this line is that it refers to the pious ones of old who used to sit for an hour before even beginning to pray the regular prayers. They were meditating and contemplating God. This suggests that despite the strong foundation the Siddur provides, establishing a vital relationship to God often requires of us other kinds of spiritual work.

Women actually have much more flexibility, within the framework of halacha, to define the kind of prayer that works for them, simply because they are not obligated to daven as much of the regular services, nor at set times.[7] Down through the centuries women have written their own prayers and poems of praise, of which, unfortunately, relatively few examples have survived.[8] One great resource of women, however, has

been the books of *Tehillim* or Psalms. Pious Jews have long recited these 150 songs, in whole or in part, on special occasions or as a personal devotion. But women have especially favored them; a grandmother will still give her young granddaughter a book of Tehillim as a very special gift. Some groups of women (or women and men) have formed "Tehillim Clubs" for the Shabbat before Rosh Chodesh, sharing the spiritual work of saying the whole book of Tehillim as is the custom of many pious Jews. This special feeling that women have for the psalms comes, I think, from the fact that their themes are often more congenial to women than are the formal prayers. They speak of concrete situations in which King David found himself rescued from distress, or they praise God's handiwork in nature. Personal, poetic, and oriented toward real life, a psalm can combine praise, inspiration, and petition into one meditation.

Jewish tradition has developed many other resources for individuals seeking a more personal relationship with God and a clearer inner sight. Phrases, verses, or whole sections of the written prayers or the psalms are often used as a focus for comtemplation or visualization. By contemplation, I mean focusing on certain thoughts that come out of one's reading, examining and working to understand and integrate them—for example, thoughts concerning God's mercy or God's greatness beyond anything we can conceive. This kind of practice is common in many Chassidic traditions, and is taught particularly in Chabad-Lubavitch. Many Chassidim have the practice of studying a mystical text for an hour before davening, so that by contemplating its meaning their prayer will be enriched. Visualization, alternatively, uses single images rather than thoughts: focusing one's mind on the letter *alef*, for example, or on an image suggested by some Torah teaching.

Another direction is the development of the whole purpose of the Amidah itself: direct talking to God. Breslov Chassidic teachings especially emphasize the practice of speaking to God in one's own language and idiom, telling one's intense concerns, expressing whatever feelings arise. Known as *hitbodedut*, this is a regular daily meditation practice (twenty to sixty minutes each day at the beginning) which, like the other practices, develops concentration, focus, and comfort in being with one's own inner self rather than involved in the busyness of daily activity. More than the others, however, the primary focus is on developing an ongoing and intense personal relationship to God.

Jewish mystics have taken the practice of meditation in other directions as well, developing higher states of consciousness more divorced from the world. Rabbi Aryeh Kaplan, following the Ralbag (Rabbi Levi ben Gershom, fourteenth century), writes of this further development of meditation as

the isolation of consciousness to an extent where it is no longer disturbed by the imagination. The imagination to which he [the Ralbag] refers is the normal reverie involving the stream of consciousness and visual imagery that is experienced when all the other senses are shut off. It is from this that the intellect [or, better, mind] must be isolated, until the individual enters a state of pure consciousness, disturbed by neither reverie nor visual imagery.[9]

To accomplish this, mystics at various times have included most of the different techniques one finds in other meditation traditions—focusing on the breath, specific body postures, meditating on letters or sounds. Intense and extended contemplation of nature was one of the preferred methods of the more rationalist medieval philosophers. Meditating on the names of God, or on their letters in various combinations, was a specialty of many of the Kabbalists. In general, however, the aim was what Rabbi Kaplan described: to divorce the mind from ordinary thoughts and to develop the ability to stay for increasing lengths of time in a clear, unimpeded state of consciousness.

These resources are important because, if we are serious about spiritual development, we eventually discover that we must learn to "sit in God's house," to allow our conscious, controlling minds to take a vacation, to focus instead on deeper inner levels, and to develop our own modes of communication with God. We find we must create time and space for quieting oneself and davening, and to stay with a practice until it bears fruit. Here the very flexibility that tradition provides for women sometimes does not serve us: with no clock-time requirements, we must provide the yoke of discipline ourselves.

One of the great aids, however, is Torah practice itself, which provides additional dimensions of order, direction, and quietude in our lives. Most of our hindrances are mental creations—whether habits like spending hours shopping or losing oneself in mystery novels, or emotional disturbances that repeatedly take over our lives. Many aspects of a Torah life gradually and quietly transform our minds, so that they no longer create so many diversions and distractions from our relationship with God. Then serious inner work becomes possible.

Perhaps the greatest aid is being in the spiritual company of other Jews. The seeds of connection to God that were planted long ago in the revelation at Mount Sinai sprout more readily in community, when we are willing for that to happen. Admittedly, many Jewish groups run from serious spirituality rather than nurturing it. But in my experience it takes only a slight turn of the head—a small bending from our famous and all-too-familiar stiff-necked attitude—for the divine gates to open wide. And being among Torah-observant Jews, once one gets beyond strangeness and fears, annoyance and stereotypes, makes possible a clear sight that one cannot always obtain on one's own.

Yet it would be naive to ignore the fact that, in Judaism as a whole, much remains to be done in the area of deep and serious spiritual development. Few teachers in any of the standard synagogue settings emphasize the contemplative side of Jewish tradition. They tend to emphasize study and action, without much instruction as to how to cultivate an inner life, often without even any acknowledgment that Ruach Hakodesh (the Holy Spirit) is a Jewish idea. This is an element of spiritual practice that modern Americans are demanding more frequently, thanks largely to exposure to Eastern religions. As women we too must ask for whatever teachings in this area our tradition offers and develop ways of cultivating it in ourselves. Certainly it is an area where women can help each other: gathering together for Torah study, forming self-help groups to deal with specific issues, learning to read the Siddur and other devotional works, meditating together. While we also need our solitude, women's communities are important to help us build inner strength.

This is part too of a more general movement of spiritual renewal in Judaism. Older and newer Chassidic groups, outreach organizations of various kinds, informal groups to celebrate together all are part of an attempt to rediscover the value of Jewish practice. Serious spiritual work among women, individually and communally, is even more recent. In a few cases, women coming together for spiritual practice has led to a direct confrontation with halacha or, at least, with established custom. At the same time, other groups go on quietly and unobtrusively, making enormous contributions to women's conscious development in spirituality. Where these will lead is yet unknown, but we can be confident that so long as it is a search for God, it will lead to good. As we ask God in the Yom Kippur prayers: "Give good hope to those who seek you, and confident speech to those who yearn for you." Women are becoming more active seekers, yearners, hopers, and speakers in our day.

Part 3

JUDAISM AND FEMINISM

Thus far I have written largely in a positive vein about Judaism and Jewish practice for women. Yet, as most readers are well aware, women have directed serious critiques against Judaism in recent years, critiques usually connected with the feminist movement in modern culture. Feminist thinkers have developed some coherent and compelling intellectual positions that have bearing on our understanding of spirituality in general and Judaism in particular.

Most people unfamiliar with the area assume that feminists are all what we might call hard-liners, emphasizing the equality of sexes in virtually all areas of life and claiming that the differences between men and women are insignificant. Proponents of this view would argue that all of human society, from family life to international affairs, can be organized on the basis of complete egalitarianism. However, in psychology and religious thought, this is not the dominant viewpoint of recent studies. More and more feminist scholars hold that, while equality is a primary value, significant differences between the genders do exist. It has long been recognized by some schools of psychology, notably the Jungian, that gender differences are relevant psychologically in understanding male and female personalities and in the healing processes that can enable a person to come to full self-realization. Recent studies point out in addition that gender differences also influence attitudes, the formation of moral judgments, and the acquisition of knowledge.[1]

These studies lend support to the feminist claim that all the disciplines of knowledge and most professions based on them are at present defined in terms of masculine values. Human society cannot appropriately include women until feminine values, attitudes, and forms of knowing are equally appreciated and institutionalized. Many feminists go much further, asserting that the dominant masculine values have corrupted our culture, leading to racism, nuclear proliferation, violence against women, and ecological crisis. Because of this, the masculine values must be overturned in favor of feminine ones.[2]

Women working in these areas are gradually developing a feminist perspective on society that promises to have great impact in the decades to come. Their studies will have implications for our understanding of feminine spirituality as well. While we can only make a preliminary assessment here, since the work is only in its early stages, it is appropriate to look at the extent to which these perspectives are compatible with Judaism's traditional view of women. Is Judaism being bypassed by new understandings of women? Or can we as Jewish women be in fruitful dialogue with modern views, so that we can use our strengths and correct our weaknesses to make a viable Jewish life for our daughters of the twenty-first century? I think the latter is the case, and in the next two chapters I will suggest how.

CHAPTER 7

Voices in Counterpoint

The realm of mystery tells us,
You live in a world full of light and life. . . .
Be attached to the legions of living beings
who are constantly bringing forth everything beautiful.
In every corner where you turn,
you are dealing with realities that have life;
you always perform consequential acts,
abounding with meaning
and with the preciousness of vibrant life.
In everything you do
you encounter sparks full of life and light,
aspiring to rise toward the heights.
*You help them and they help you.**

Women in the twentieth century are "finding their voices." This is perhaps the great theme of modern women's lives: we who have been silent
are speaking out, describing ourselves, our experiences, our points of
view in our own ways rather than—as in the past—having no voice at all
or having our ideas filtered through the speech and writings of men. In
religious thought—and here we will be referring to modern Christian and

---

* Abraham Isaac Kook, "The Glory of Life," in *The Lights of Penitence, the Moral Principles,*
Lights of Holiness, Essays, Letters, and Poems, trans. Ben Zion Bokser (New York: Paulist
Press, 1978), p. 223.

Jewish thought unless otherwise noted—this has resulted in a dramatic awakening and the development of ideas that sometimes seem to have the potential of reconstructing our ways of thinking altogether. Women are attempting to write in new styles and even create words that better convey our experiences and meanings. Women from various ethnic groups—blacks, American Indians, Asian Americans as well as Jews—are offering their perspectives and their inherited wisdom to the effort of clarifying women's reflection on experience.

We cannot consider the whole range of feminist thought here. We will be able to touch on only a few areas that in my opinion are the most crucial for Jewish women's self-understanding and self-esteem. One of the things we want to know is whether—even if we love Jewish tradition and practice—we are buying into a system that undercuts our full humanity, our full womanhood. Many Jewish feminists believe that we (along with women in most other religious traditions) cannot participate with integrity in our tradition unless we make radical changes. Although, as we have already seen, there are many elements in our tradition that are richly relevant to women and positive for our growth, they could argue that we are fooling ourselves. Perhaps these are marginal features, while the core of tradition remains misogynist and oppressive to women. This issue needs to be addressed directly.

The way I have chosen to approach the question is to examine some of the leading writings in feminist religious thought. Many feminists are finding fundamental currents in women's spirituality that seem to appear cross-culturally and that have been opposed, denigrated, or forced underground by male dominance in religion. They have also found persistent habits of thought—basic philosophical assumptions about the nature of things—that are negative toward women and our kinds of spirituality. We must examine the extent to which these negative elements are present in Judaism and whether Jewish tradition allows and encourages women's self-expression in positive, significant ways.[1]

To begin with fundamentals: one of the most important and recurrent issues discussed in feminist literature is the dualistic framework of Western religious thought that associates the feminine with negative characteristics. Most Western philosophical and religious thinkers assume a division between spirit and matter, or mind and body, such that spirit and mind are superior to matter and body. Further, the male is associated with spirit, the female with matter. This is worked out in a series of correlated oppositions reflected in many varieties of religious thought. Here is a partial list:

spirit / matter	intellect / senses
mind / body	God / human beings
transcendence / immanence	reason/emotion
supernatural / natural	male / female

In almost every case the first of the two is presented as superior, the second as inferior.

A second major issue has to do with the standards set for development along the spiritual path. As has been discovered by Gilligan, Belenky, and colleagues in the areas of morality and knowledge, so in spirituality: desirable goals are male, stressing independence, solitariness, and individual mastery. The lone ascetic in his cell, the prophet on a mountaintop, and the charismatic leader of a religious organization all emphasize the singular individual and achieving a place at the top of a hierarchy. Feminists suggest that while we may value our private communion with God, women's spirituality is essentially relational, as is expressed in one of the movement's favorite images: weaving webs of relations between self and other selves, self and world. How the experience of the individual interfaces with the networks of others is one of the cutting edges of feminist thought. But it is clear that a strongly relational orientation prevails, giving feminine spirituality a definite communal and moral/ethical bent from the beginning.

A third, related issue is the role of emotion in self and mind. Feminists tend to reject pure intellectual analysis for a more engaged, involved, or personal style. This brings us back again to the oppositions that are inherent in much of Western thought: mind and reason are usually pitted against emotion and sensuality, with reason being taken as the ultimate arbiter in human affairs. Feminists argue that cutting ourselves off from emotion and feeling has created forms of spirituality that are inadequate, unsatisfying, and ultimately unethical.

These problems are, as we will see, interrelated, but let us take them one by one before we weave them together. First, the feminist struggle with the inherited dualistic categories of Western thought—the oppositions cited above—goes back at least to Simone de Beauvoir's *The Second Sex* (1949), in which she developed an existentialist critique of Western culture's oppression of women. She showed how woman and the feminine are habitually regarded as being on the side of nature, the body, the irrational, and, theologically, "immanence." She insisted that women must refuse to accept these male definitions and regard themselves instead as "transcendent subjects"—creative and not merely receptive, initiating and not treated as an object, the Other.[2] This means that we must affirm our freedom as creative individuals, using that liberty to move "outward, forward, and upward," as Catherine Keller puts it, a privilege men had hoarded for themselves.[3] De Beauvoir's influence on feminism has been enormous, and most subsequent feminist thinkers accepted her critique of Western society.

Recently, however, another view has emerged. Here works like Susan Griffin's *Woman and Nature* (1978) have been extremely powerful. Griffin and others affirm that the feminine is indeed deeply connected with "nature" and "immanence," as de Beauvoir held, but this is not negative: embodiment is part of our deeply feminine mode of being. Creativity emerges from our bodies, from our physical nature, and our finite limitations, not in negation of them. We must affirm these deeply natural parts of ourselves and at the same time undercut the negative force of the dualistic system. Rosemary Radford Reuther, who sees the "dualism of nature and transcendence, matter and spirit as female against male" as "basic to male theology," insists that both sides must be rejected: "mother-matter-matrix as 'static immanence'" and "spirit and transcendence as rootless, antinatural, originating in an 'other world' beyond the cosmos."[4] Catherine Keller undercuts the dichotomy in another way. She suggests that de Beauvoir herself bought into the male definition of women and "women's work" in the world and that the concept of the transcendent subject was simply a cultural projection, the "perennial 'male ego.'" In her view, our feminine sense of connection, relationship, and responsibility can provide a ground of identity and action that does not require buying into male forms of alienation and aggression.[5]

The feminist revaluation of immanence is most clearly articulated in writings concerning women's intuited connection with the world, our sense of being inseparably a part of nature and the universe. Many have found compelling Alice Walker's characterization of women's spirituality in *The Color Purple,* when her character Shug describes herself as having "that feeling of being part of everything, not separate at all. I knew that if I cut a tree, my arm would bleed." Most traditional Western religious thinkers — Jewish as well as Christian — would regard such a view as heading toward pantheism, theologically mistaken and, because it has no transcendent source, offering no basis for morality. But Carol P. Christ suggests we can affirm morality even if we do not affirm a transcendent God beyond nature, even if we conceive of God as an impersonal natural process:

Let us entertain the possibility that the divinity that shapes our ends is an impersonal process of life, death, and transformation . . . that the life force does not care more about human creativity and choice than it cares about the ability of bermuda grass to spread or moss to form on the side of a tree. . . . Does it therefore follow that there is no reason for humans not to destroy a universe that has been created through aeons of life, death, and transformation? I suggest that what can stop us is not knowledge that our self-reflection and freedom are in the image of God, nor that self-sacrifice is in the image of Christ. What can stop us, I propose, is a deeply felt connection to all beings in the web of life. What can stop us is that we love this life, this earth, the joy we know in ourselves and other beings enough to find the thought of the end of the earth intolerable. We do not need to know that our moral will is in the image of a personal God in order to know that we have the capacity to create death or to love and preserve life.[6]

Christ goes on to say that we need not conceive of this "web of life" as necessarily uncaring or unfeeling; but even if we do, we have a ground for morality in our own love of life. She echoes here de Beauvoir's sentiment: "If we do not love life on our own account and through others, it is futile to seek to justify it in any way."[7]

We can see here how the feminist emphasis on immanence, undercutting what women have experienced as an oppressive dualism, connects with two other aspects of women's thought: relatedness, that is, an inner sense of connection, and reliance on feeling as a ground for judgment and knowledge. If the universe is conceived of as simply the arena of fixed natural law, or as nature wild and untamed, it gives us no ground for moral judgments—one needs a transcendent lawmaker who provides laws for both nature and human beings and some mode, beyond nature, of implanting morality in the human being. But in Carol Christ's view, it is relatedness, love and caring, a felt connection with other beings that provide, within our human nature, reasons for acting morally. This felt relationship is fundamental to women's spirituality. As she and Judith Plaskow write, the feminist sense of the self "is essentially relational, inseparable from the limiting and enriching contexts of body, feeling, relationship, community, history, and the web of life. The notion of the relational self can be correlated with the immanent turn in feminist views of the sacred: in both cases connection to that which is finite, changing, and limited is affirmed."[8] Over against the philosopher Descartes, whose famous "I think, therefore I am" described the rational, disembodied, solitary ego, the feminine self is embodied, passionate, relational, communal. From this point of view, religious thinkers who talk about God as "being itself" or the "wholly other"—or in Judaism those who translate *Adonai echad* as "God is uniquely alone"—imply that God's lack of relatedness is a source of strength.[9] For feminists only that divinity which is deeply related in and to the world can be authentic.

Feelings are fundamental here as well, not only the intuition of connection or relationship, but also personal feelings of joy, love, sensuality, sadness. Deep feelings are a guide to action because they are signals of inner truth. For example, Beverly Wildung Harrison suggests that anger is a "feeling-signal" that can be the beginning of a moral guide, for it is "a sign of some resistance in ourselves to the moral quality of the social relations in which we are immersed."[10] Feelings of love and joy are signals of the affirmation of life, as Carol Christ sees it: "To seek to perpetuate and preserve life because we enjoy it, because we love it, seems to me to be more life-affirming than the somewhat ascetic notion of 'service to God' and the somewhat masochistic notion of 'radical self-giving.' . . . Such love must inspire an ethic rooted in a desire to enhance the life possibilities of all beings, both human and nonhuman."[11] To reject the use of feelings as a guide in favor of rational precepts is, she suggests in this passage, "ascetic" or "masochistic." Our traditional rationalist asceticism stands in contrast to Walker's character Shug, who says, "God love all them feelings." Harrison explains this point of view more fully:

All our knowledge, including our moral knowledge, is body-mediated knowledge. All knowledge is rooted in our sensuality. . . . If feeling is damaged or cut off, our power to image the world and act into it is destroyed and our rationality is impaired. Our power to value the world gives way as well. . . . This is why psychotherapy has to be understood as a very basic form of moral education. . . . Failure to live deeply in "our bodies, ourselves" destroys the possibility of moral relations between us.[12]

For these writers, relationships, connection to nature, and immanence all intertwine in their understanding of feminine spirituality.

Such features are not at all alien to what our tradition has handed down about Jewish women and the feminine (see again p. 48). In our discussion of ritual, we saw that woman's connection to nature is a persistent element. Feminine heroines and theme are strongly associated with the seasonal cycles; and women are associated with the moon, with motherhood, with food and nurturing, and with nature's sexual cycles. Whether in holidays like Rosh Chodesh or special mitzvot like challah and niddah, women bring a spiritual dimension to the practical, real-life, finite embodiment of human beings.

Jewish women's life also emphasizes relationships and relatedness, with a strong connection to the concrete and personal aspects of life and a sense of interdependence. Women's traditional affinity for Tehillim (Psalms) suggests an appreciation both for nature and for personal, related spirituality—King David's intimate relation with God through all his various hardships and victories had great appeal. The women of our stories too were deeply concerned with relationships—first with family, particularly with husbands and children, then with the larger destiny of their descendants and the Jewish people as a whole.

We observed also that the very idea of motherhood in this tradition carries a strong sense of responsibility for the future: the women knew their actions would shape destiny. Jewish women were not trapped in "static immanence." On the contrary, the woman "looks smilingly to the future" and exerts her power to shape it. We saw that women often took risks and did the unconventional. Indeed, the stories of Jewish women suggest the truth of the description of premodern women given by Beverly Harrison when she says, "Historically, I believe, women have always exemplified the power of activity over passivity, of experimentation over routinization, of creativity and risk-taking over conventionality."[13]

Jewish women are portrayed as oriented toward the immanent, the practical, and the web of relations for which they have considerable responsibility. Yet we are not simply immersed in material concerns. Jewish tradition sees us as essentially inward beings, whose essence revolves around the private sphere. The saying "All the glory of the daughter of the king is on the inside" focuses on that inwardness. That woman is the ruler of Shabbat, the day of inward orientation—toward home, community, and personal spirituality—exemplifies this also. On a personal level Channah as the model for prayer is an example: a woman deeply connected to her feelings expressing herself to God. In the prophetic consciousness of Sarah, Rivkah, and others we also see a strong inwardness: women had their own base of knowledge that came from within. Tamar, Yehudit, and Esther all acted outside the boundaries of what was usually considered proper and right on the basis of their inner moral certainty. Thus Judaism has recognized the inner strength of women and extolled it as a feminine virtue. This actually deepens what feminists have said about basing our knowledge and morality on our inner sense of things, including our feelings and intuitions. Jewish tradition suggests that, beyond feelings and emotions, feminine consciousness can operate at a level that approaches the prophetic. (We will consider below some additional thoughts about this dimension.)

There are some other arguments to be heard, however. Some feminists have claimed that while there may be feminine dimensions to Jewish religious life, they are not really valued in Judaism—synagogue, yeshiva, and law court are more important. From an experiential point of view, many women and men within traditional Judaism will affirm that this is simply not so. Torah life is a total way of life, with women's responsibilities just as serious as men's, and equally highly valued. The question perhaps is whether women have appreciated the importance of affirming this dimension of their lives and speaking publicly about it. In the past most of the life of women remained private. In modern times, as traditional communities disintegrated, Jewish women's occupations—as with other women—were denigrated and in addition were subject to the general Enlightenment criticism of obsolete ritual. It is only in recent times that women involved in traditional practice have begun to break the silence about their experience.

Another aspect of the patriarchal appearance of Judaism is that women's spirituality has often not been formally organized. Connections among women themselves have been implicit rather than explicit. When we look at the stories of women, we find a great deal of family experience but almost no stories of women with other women—Ruth and Naomi are the exception. There are hints of women's networks—the women who collaborated against Pharaoh to hide Jewish children, who refused en masse to give their jewelry to make the golden calf. But such networks have been largely invisible. We may well imagine that they simply seemed unimportant to the males who wrote the stories, but we may also assume that they were informal and loosely organized, as has often been customary and comfortable among women.

However, we must recognize that when women's efforts were coordinated by casual word of mouth or meetings at the river to do laundry, women did not learn—or did not have confidence in their learning—to speak out, to become "public" people, to speak on behalf of others. As long as Jewish tradition was strong, they could perhaps pass on the values they cherished and the way their spirituality worked for them in a "hidden" way. But in the long run, with the breakdown of communities, women's values became merely private, not part of our general heritage. Moreover, when faced by truly repressive acts, whether male violence or men's verbal denigration of women, the traditional informal network could become sheer ineffectiveness. Some feminine modes of action can become yielding acquiescence rather than confrontation. Only since a strong feminist movement emerged has that begun to change, revealing that women are not only private, inward beings but that they also have a way of bonding with one another that has enormous potential in the public realm.

Even if we grant the strengths of Jewish women in the past, there is still more to the feminist argument: Is it not true that underneath the positive features we find in Judaism a negative valuation of women or of the feminine principle? Do not the spirit / matter, soul / body, transcendent / immanent polarities appear in Jewish thought in ways detrimental to the feminine side? They do; but differently than in Greek or Christian thought. In Jewish mystical thought, for example, we often find man or the masculine associated with spirit, woman with body; then body is associated with the "animal," and this in turn with the temptations that turn a person away from God. While Judaism never castigated Chava (Eve) and all women in the way Christianity did for bringing on the first sin, still the literature is laced with associations of the feminine to our animal nature and thus to spiritual danger. At the same time, Judaism has affirmed more consistently than Christianity a positive attitude toward body, nature, and world. Male and female are always seen as interdependent, though the male—particularly male anatomy—is the mystical model of humanity. Moreover, women are regarded as more spiritual than men. But it is clear that Judaism has absorbed to some degree the dualistic presuppositions of Western—particularly Greek—thought that tend to devalue the feminine.

Another example: the two names of God most frequently used in the Bible, "Adonai" and "Elohim," are associated with the masculine and feminine, respectively. The first is connected to the aspect of God that expresses mercy, redemption, and the assertion of God's benign will acting from outside the universe as we know it. The second, feminine aspect is associated with nature, fixed law, the eternal round of things. The first is dynamic: God's action in history that makes possible new events, new revelations. The second, feminine, appears static, moving in eternal circles. In Judaism this second aspect of God expresses justice as well—the more severe side of God that, like nature, moves in terms of fixed laws of reward and punishment.

Let us look more closely at what is at stake here. First: can we have a more benign and intimate perception of God by eliminating the idea of transcendence with its masculine associations? It would seem not. From the traditional Jewish point of view, one cannot collapse the transcendence of God into the immanence of nature. The two dimensions are absolutely essential. If one had only a transcendent God, one would have an evil, or at best a neutral and mechanical, world. But if one had only an immanent God, taking the world of nature as divine, as feminists like Carol Christ wish to do, one would collapse into paganism. Nature has divinity within it, to be sure, but that is secondary, dependent on the transcendent Creator God who formed nature and gave it its fixed laws. God is immanent in the world, but that world is totally dependent for its existence on the continually acting transcendent will, the consciousness that lies beyond nature. (Translate: the feminine is entirely dependent for her creative power on the masculine.) Similarly, the transcendent God gave the Torah as the fixed system of laws for human beings. That same transcendent divine will which guides nature is the source of all guidelines for human action: the mitzvot and morality itself. His Torah given on Sinai is our guide, not any inner intuitions from the Shekhinah. (Translate: the masculine is the source of all morality.)

Yet part of the problem is our understanding of the word *transcendence*. Its common meaning is that which is above the limits of human thought—beyond good and evil, beyond mind and emotion, beyond male and female. In various usages, however, it takes on different connotations. As we observed, in much of Western thought it has become attached to mind / spirit / reason as opposed to body / matter / emotion. But, in another context, the literary "transcendentalists" used the term to connote a kind of higher intuition, a Reason above ordinary rational logic. The term is itself subject to much confusion. We should take transcendence to mean that which precedes any levels of being or intelligence than we, in our human finitude, can know.

But we must understand this in a Jewish context. Our idea of transcendence derives from religious experiences different from those of the Greeks, who, from Plato on down, emphasized the split between spirit and matter. The primary experience that for Jewish tradition gave rise to the concept of transcendence, the name "Adonai," was the exodus from Egypt, God's redemption of the Jewish people. "Ask if any deed as mighty as this has been seen or heard!" exclaimed Moses. "Did ever a God attempt to come and take a nation for himself out of another nation, . . . as the Lord your God did for you in Egypt in the sight of all of you?" (Deut. 4.32–34) Rabbi Abraham Isaac Kook wrote that human "sovereignty over the world's lower creatures with an idealistic motivation"—that is, our moral sense of responsibility—"began to be manifested in the miracles and wonders of the exodus from Egypt, which stamped the Jewish people with its historic character."[14] From the unfathomable work of God in redeeming a group of slaves first came the Jewish view that God transcends the world; for it was here, according to traditional thought, that God exceeded anything known in nature. God performed miracles to overturn nature and human rulership, to liberate the Israelite slaves.[15]

Rosemary Reuther has pointed out many respects in which the Israelite God transcended "patriarchal consciousness." Calling Abraham away from his father's house, breaking the bonds between the overlord Pharaoh and his subjects signified that rules of father and son, master and slave, king and subject could be broken to establish a higher allegiance, an allegiance formed from love. Moreover, God did this in response to the "crying out" of the slaves. It was an act of mercy, not on the basis of merit.[16]

Another way of putting this is that justice did not require the miraculous redemption of the slaves; it could not be explained in ordinary rational terms. From the point of view of "nature," the slaves should have had to work out what might be called their karma. Their actions in the past had borne this fruit; as with all actions, we reap their reward or punishment.[17] But the God who intervenes in this eternal round of justice can change the course of things—can, as we mentioned in the last chapter, respond to a person's repentance, can forgive, can show mercy even if it is not deserved. It makes no sense, in nature's terms, or in terms of rational justice, that good deeds should be remembered for a thousand generations, and evil ones only to the third and fourth (Exod. 33:7). But that is the way of God according to Judaism.

The point of view represented in Torah, prophets, and classical rabbinic interpretations holds that it is God's mercy—not his thought, mind, intellect, spirit, logos, or other Greek philosophical characteristics—that exemplifies his transcendence, because it comes from a place beyond the natural order of things. God, in Jewish thought from the Exodus down to modern times, is unimaginably loving, giving, compassionate, beneficent. As the great seventeenth-century thinker, Moshe Chaim Luzzato, taught, God's purpose in creation is to give of his goodness to his creatures.

But this is precisely what feminists demand of God: that s/he be related, compassionate, bountiful. Part of the natural feminine moral sensibility is to recognize bonds of love—between parent and child, man and woman, friend and friend, and even between strangers—which connect us all together. We see nature as interdependent and mutually supportive. We experience relations between people, as Carol Gilligan has pointed out, as matters of care, responsibility, and responsiveness, not primarily the balancing of claims according to rules of justice. These are all reflected in the way women experience God. And these same elements infuse the Jewish view of God: when we ask why God redeemed the Hebrew slaves, the Torah tells us that he heard their cries. It is an eminently feminine answer. One can argue that the Jewish people had merit—merit as Abraham's descendents, merit for maintaining their Jewish lives in the midst of Egyptian culture. But most simply, God heard their cries—like a mother whose child is crying, he could not let it go on any longer. So it is understandable that many women students ask me why "Adonai," the name of God representing mercy, should be male—

shouldn't this be the female side of God? For they know this mercy as part of feminine experience.

So, of course, do men, on their female side. And it is God's transcendent compassion that Judaism attempts to embody in *halacha*, the same compassion that women find rooted in their own intuitions of relatedness. Understood from a Jewish perspective, then, divine transcendence bridges across the supposedly male and female views. The one who redeems slaves, the one who carries the people to freedom as an eagle carries its young on its wings (Exod. 19:4, Deut. 32:11), the one who inspires Moses to care for them as a nursing father(!)—this divinity is intimately related to our lives. We are called to an *imitatio dei*, to be like this God in responding to the needs of the widow, the orphan, the slave, the stranger. In the practical realm this has meant, on the one hand, enacting laws, the halacha, and applying them with care and compassion; and on the other hand, developing the knowledge and character that come from the depth of our being, reflected in the stories, the aggadah, of the great women and men of our tradition. Here halacha and aggadah unite; our Torah is one.

Yet we are not done with our Greek influences. We must look afresh at the concept of God that we have inherited from Genesis: that God is the Creator who makes the world *ex nihilo*, from nothing, and is totally independent of creation. Many feminists charge that this is another dimension of transcendence which emphasizes God's unrelatedness to us. They are attracted to myths of other cultures wherein a female deity creates the world from her own body or where the things of the world spring forth from a feminine earth. In contrast, Jewish tradition insists on the independence of the creator God who creates by his word. This later became connected with Greek concepts of transcendence, spirit, mind, and reason, setting up the full range of dichotomies we have discussed above. Also related are the emphasis on God's eternal, unchanging nature and on God as "uniquely alone." It is but a step from this to putting male (spirit / thought / creator) above female (nature / body / creation) in hierarchical fashion.

I agree with feminist theologians that we must do away with the insufferable philosophical dualism that puts women at the bottom. In fact, dualism is unnecessary if we recognize that, for us as Jews, two things are at stake: our understanding of God as totally free of limitations, absolutely free to create, and the idea that we partake of this freedom in some degree even though we, unlike God, have limitations. Since we are made in God's image, in some respect we are like God. The problem is, the part that is like God is described, in most of Western tradition, as our spirit, soul, or mind. What is left over—body, flesh, animal self—then is regarded as not like God. This is the root of the difficulty.

Having a thinking machine in our brains or an incorporeal soul residing somewhere inside does not make us like God. Rather it is in freedom of the *will*, soul freedom, that we are like God. We have the capacity to act beyond our nature, to change ourselves, to decide and act in any moment. It is often taught that the seat of the soul is in the mind or brain. This makes it sound as if the soul (and therefore the will) is primarily a thinking entity, a rationalist creation. But this is not the case. The soul is the seat of the will. The mind or brain may formulate that will into what we recognize as "thought," but it is the will that originates any decision or nonhabitual action—the will that is beyond the mind.

Feminist thinkers, frustrated with the frequent masculine insistence on the primacy of thought, suggest an alternative: that the root of our will is not rational thought but feeling—feeling understood in the broadest sense as our experienced, embodied relation to the world and in the deepest sense as our intuition. Yet most Jewish moral perspectives hold that feelings are not a good guide to morality. They may be honored as signals of happiness or distress, but they are essentially selfish and must be trained and curbed in order not to run to excess. Anger, for example, is regarded in rabbinic tradition as an expression of idolatry—idolatry of the self. Love, while it may appear altruistic, is often a mask for self-love. Even positive feelings connected with religion cannot be trusted as certain guides to spiritual development. They may only tempt one into pride and self-satisfaction. In most ethical and Chassidic texts, the theme is rehearsed that one cannot trust one's feelings very far; only the revelation of Torah from God, as it has been passed on through authentic tradition, can give proper guidance.

Some feminists do recognize, in passing, the possibility of too much reliance on feelings. Harrison, while stressing the importance of feelings in our moral perceptions, also acknowledges that feelings do not necessarily lead to "wise or humane action."[18] Catherine Keller also recognizes that the love expressed in the "almost animistic" idea of inseparability from other beings and things "is vulnerable to criticisms of solipsism, narcissism, and stagnation."[19] Then, we may ask, where do wisdom and humanity to guide our actions come from? Are we then forced to return to the intellectualist tradition that insists on the supremacy of thought and the rejection of feelings?

Jewish tradition answers that the matter is complex: mind, body, emotion are all involved. As the sages of rabbinic times said, "The kidneys advise, the heart understands" (Berachot 61a).[20] We could argue long over how we as human beings actually work—how our will comes to be active in the world and how our will can best be opened to the right way of action. It is possible that men and women experience this differently in the intricate intermingling of body, mind, and emotion. In any case, what we learn—and this is verified over and over again in the experience of the observant Jew—is that this complex wisdom is most fully embodied in our inherited body of tradition, mediated through the words of our teachers.

Specifically, we must insist, through the *words* of our teachers. Let us remind ourselves of the picture we are given in Genesis of God the Creator. God's distinctive characteristic—which he passes on to those made in his image—is that of Speaker, the Speaker-Who-Creates, the one who brings things into being by speaking them. This is an aspect of God's transcendence: what is not part of nature, not part of the round of birth and rebirth, of karmic or natural law. We are not told anything about God's thoughts or feelings here. Speech is the mode in which, so far as we can know, the Divine Will comes into being; it manifests God's freedom to create.

This is so for us as well. Speech has a freedom, a "transcendence" that the rest of nature does not have. Communication goes on among the rest of the creatures, but speech in the creative sense does not—or at least not without humans to help it come to voice. Yet we need not make this Creative Speech into the Greek *logos*, with its platonic associations of detached rationality. Plato regarded poetry and drama as decidedly inferior to philosophy; as a result, much of our Western philosophical heritage separated pure thought, and speech as its vehicle, from feeling, intuition, dream, vision, physicality. As Jews we can leave Plato behind and recover our own ways of speaking—in ritual, song, poetry, story, prophecy as well as reasoned discourse.

Again, the Jewish dual tradition is important: halacha—the speech of rationality and logic—and aggadah—the speech of story, dream, vision—never were entirely separated. The Talmud, our great classic compilation of oral law, mixes the two throughout. In practice the handing down of the law always should be from person to person, teacher to student, Rav to questioner—an ongoing dialogue, not merely laws read from books. Judaism has been, to borrow Plaskow's terms, "passionate, communal, embodied." But historically, as the speech of halacha became dominant, beginning with the monarchy and exile and increasing enormously in the Greco-Roman period, less came from the feminine side. Women, once visionaries and prophetesses, spoke less in the public realm as the centuries passed.

Now women are recovering, taking back their share of the power of speech. Women's midrash, women's prayers, women's inspiration are rising once again; and as women become engaged in the creative work of public speech, it will affect all of Jewish life, including halacha. This is the way to address the issue of dualism—not by philosophical arguments on behalf of the importance of feelings, but by what we speak. It will become apparent through our speech that our bodies also speak truth, that our feelings and intuitions can interact with Torah learning to provide guides to action. Speaking out is taking part in the creative act by which God continues to bring new things into the world, to act with compassion and caring, in ways beyond what we as women have done before. And we do this from the place of immanence, from our connection to the divine hiddenness, from our knowledge of the Shekhinah, of Rachel weeping with us. And we ask men to call back to their consciousness the knowledge of immanence: that they too are created bodies, they must speak from feeling, they must make their creative work in the world compassionate, related, feminine.[21]

The feminine has much to say in Jewish tradition, and the years ahead promise stimulating dialogue between the community of women and that of men. This brings us to the final point. Too often when we speak as feminists we set up another "we-they" dichotomy, objectifying men in our speech as they have done to us in so many ways. But if we truly live in a relational world, where each is part of the other, men are part of us too, both inwardly in our androgynous psyches and in the web of life in which we move. The universe, according to our Jewish understanding, rests on the delicate balance of male and female, one that we must work out in our families, our communities, and the public world. As I mentioned above, *Adonai echad*—God is one—does not need to mean, "God is uniquely alone." God's oneness, the divine unity, is the marriage of female and male, the transcendent union that is neither mind nor body, spirit nor matter, nor anything else we can comprehend. For us it means we seek the unity of inner knowing and soaring mind, creative speech and compassionate wisdom from within ourselves and among ourselves, in community.

CHAPTER 8

Listening to Her Voice

Shema —
listen

Yisrael, Yashir-el —
God's song is within us.

Listen,
don't speak just yet
listen
wait
let love rise within.

If it is true that Judaism holds within it at least the the seeds of balance between the sexes—and my personal opinion is that it contains much more than this—what does that mean in the everyday realities of our communities? Feminists have argued that it doesn't mean much. Even in nontraditional branches of Judaism, men have until recently largely controlled the institutions of Judaism, from places of worship to educational institutions. Women were relegated to the sisterhoods, devoting themselves to charitable activities and maintaining the community's social life. In orthodoxy it appears even worse, with the separation of men and women in synagogues and different obligations for men and women.

As a result, feminists have urged women to take stronger leadership roles and to insist on egalitarian treatment, so that women are not excluded from anything men do and are not forced into unwelcome "female" roles. There are two areas in which the difficulties have focused. First is the synagogue, where the community gathers for ritual. (Generally, in nonritual areas of community life, women are as vocal and prominent as men, even in orthodox congregations.) Women have sought to be counted in a minyan or to become rabbis or chazzans (leaders of worship).[1] Second, women have not participated directly in the formation of halacha, principally because they have not been ordained as rabbis. Since the restriction of women in these areas often seems alien and oppressive, feminists have argued that the best thing is simply to do away with all restrictions. Nothing will work except complete egalitarianism. Anything else is simply unjust.

Injustice is a harsh charge against any Jewish movement, because justice is one of the primary values of Judaism itself. The problem is that justice always must be defined in a context—it cannot be merely abstract—and traditionalists and nontraditionalists do not agree on the context. For example, in community ritual such as davening on Shabbat, many feminists regard the synagogue as like any other community, to be operated on the model of democratic politics in modern civil society. One person, one vote, and any person can fill any role (theoretically at least; in practice dependent on desire and training). In my view, the context should be understood differently. In its ritual dimension the synagogue is a spiritual manifestation, not a political one. This means that communal worship expresses an archetype, an essential statement about human community, and this takes precedence over other functions the synagogue might have.

An example of this is the division Cohen, Levi, and Israel in the community. When the Torah is read, a Cohen (if one is present) always receives the first aliyah, and a Levi the second. On the holidays, the Cohanim all participate in blessing the people. These special roles are given simply by virtue of the family of one's birth. They do not reflect a person's level of learning, observance, wealth, or community participation. Nor does the Cohen or Levi receive any special privilege or power outside the ritual framework. But at the moment of the Torah ritual or the blessing of the people, the Cohen and the Levi are special. At that moment the community is represented in archetypal fashion as we are supposed to appear before God in the Holy Temple—Cohen, Levi, and Israel play their own roles in the spiritual drama of offering ourselves communally to God.

Similarly with the division between men and women: it expresses a spiritual dynamic that reflects no judgment as to a person's ability, learning, spiritual commitment, or secular power. The mechitzah (partition) in the synagogue is a symbolic representation of the male-female polarity that we have seen in so many areas of traditional Judaism. Many women come to love the separation, as I have, for it provides an arena of privacy free from intrusive male presence and enables women to develop a greater sense of community. But whether we love it or not, it resonates with fundamental Jewish values. Judaism states over and over again that male and female are basic to the construction of the universe: Adam and Chava, Abraham and Sarah, Isaac and Rivkah, Jacob and Rachel / Leah, man and wife in Egypt, all the way down to the insistence, throughout rabbinic Judaism, on the value of marriage. Partners with different functions, different life realities, women and men also have different spiritual needs and purposes, and the synagogue is the place where those manifest in community.[2]

But, precisely because this is an archetype of community—a reality operating below the level of consciousness, and one applicable to the Jewish community as a whole—it does not always satisfy an individual's conscious, immediate needs. Judaism allows for this. As individuals we may need, at certain stages in our spiritual development, some of the spiritual motivations or satisfactions that are designated primarily for the other sex. Pious women have sometimes taken on, privately, the practice of donning tallit and tefillin as men do. Individual women may take on the discipline of praying at fixed times, with a minyan. On the other side, sometimes a man may need to be released from the obligation to daven at set times or to appear at a minyan. Traditional Judaism allows for these individual differences. But the community gathered in ritual is a different matter, expressing not individual desires but the archetype—male and female in their essence.

We often fail to appreciate the complexity and power of the internal structure of traditional Judaism because so many other features of society have moved in a different direction. The traditional synagogue then appears a relic of the past—at least from outside. From inside, in a healthy community, it can be experienced as a natural structure, an extended family. The rabbi is still a master of the law, a judge in disputes, and a teacher who transmits a thoroughly Jewish way of life. The community is a learning community and a self-reflective one, practicing continual self-examination to bring their lives to higher and higher spiritual standards. The role of halacha and of rabbinic leadership in everyday practice are central here. As the sages advised, "Provide yourself a rav [rabbinic adviser] and acquire a companion [in Torah]" (Pirke Avot 1:6). A supportive community and a guide in the Jewish way of life re-create the conditions where the ritual community also makes sense.

Outside the traditional setting not only the synagogue but also the rabbinate has become something rather different. Rabbis are teachers, to be sure, but not necessarily knowledgeable in halacha; they often function more as inspiring speakers, counselors, or community organizers for Jewish causes. For idealistic, spiritually inclined Jewish women who really want to contribute to Judaism, it has seemed to make sense that the role of rabbi, as it has evolved in the present day, is a good place for them. Women often find themselves suited to teaching, counseling, and inspiration; and the rabbinate is certainly a position from which women can be heard. But now we raise the pointed question, is this the wisest way to guide our lives as individuals and as communities? To put it another way, what do we lose by opting for a leadership platform—male or female—that does not support traditional Jewish life? If I am right that traditional life preserves rich and significant values for both men and women, it may be that we are undermining ourselves.

We saw in chapter 3 that feminine spirituality in Judaism has had a different tone and quality, moving toward the prophetic/intuitive end of the spectrum and developing spirituality in the midst of daily life. In our survey of ritual practices and the inner work of prayer and study, we saw how women have found satisfying ways of connecting to God along many dimensions: vital life force, body, sexuality, the inwardness of personal devotions, study, and meditation. In chapter 7 we saw many of these same themes echoed in the religious thought of contemporary feminists. What we want is to recover, preserve, and enrich these feminine features of our spirituality in our contemporary world. We have to ask what the modern pulpit and synagogue really offer us. They offer a platform and a voice, to be sure, but is it authentically our voice? Most important, do they offer us ways to develop, in ourselves and in our communities, that intuitive, relationship-based way of life that is our feminine heritage?

There are other, healthier ways to renew ourselves as women within our Jewish communities. We must recommit to a fully Jewish way of life; and, I believe, the best definition of this life, the best outline for it, is halacha. But if synagogue ritual is a difficult point for many women, halachic process is equally so. Many feminists ask, how can women accept a halacha they have had little part in making? And how can we participate (if at all) in shaping it henceforth? The answer to the first question is simple, even though it may be emotionally difficult: we can accept halacha as guidelines for our lives, as the heritage from our mothers and fathers, with faith and trust. Today we often fear that because Jewish law has been shaped by men, it does not take women into account. But I believe that, instead of feeding this fear, we can nourish trust in our tradition—trust in the strength of the women who came before us, and trust in the inner balance which we know is at the heart of Judaism. Within this framework, we take on Jewish practice as we can, giving it a chance to mature and develop in our lives. This is both a leap of faith and an adventure into spirituality.

An answer to the second question is more complex. This is not a matter of the symbolic or ritual dimension of religion, but rather the rational one that guides our ordinary decision-making processes as we shape our lives. Thus it seems unquestionable that in some way women should be included in the halachic process. But at the same time, relatively few women have been attracted to advanced studies in Jewish law. In the past there have been times and places in Jewish history when women had opportunities to learn; yet very few took advantage of them. Only a few women—probably the most notable example is the famous Beruria, Rabbi Meir's wife in talmudic times—were regarded as able to poskin, that is, to hand down halachic decisions. Such women were greatly respected in their times, but they were rare.[3] Even today women tend to prefer studies of Chumash, midrash, and mysticism rather than advanced studies of Gemara, which is prerequisite to understanding the complexities of Jewish law.

Certainly women who wish to pursue legal studies should be permitted and encouraged to do so. But we are likely to find ourselves in the position of having a few superb women scholars as a tiny minority among men—similar, perhaps, to the proportion of female judges in the American court system. Without pressing the argument, I would simply state my doubts as to whether women will, in the near future, have a significant impact on halacha from this route.

By other means, however, women have made actual changes in halacha, often out of love for the mitzvot, in the direction of making it stricter or more binding on themselves. It is said that in talmudic times women took on themselves more stringent laws of niddah. Their custom of attending Rosh Hashanah services in order to hear the blowing of the shofar led to a change in the law: now women are considered obligated to hear the shofar, whereas in ancient times we were exempt. There are other examples. Today, certain practices of women seem likely to spread, for example, the practice of women's gatherings on Rosh Chodesh or of holding a Melava Malkah celebration ("escorting the queen," Saturday night after Shabbat) for the birth of a baby girl. This growth of private custom into widespread practice has been one important way that *minhag* has come to have in observant communities the force of law. Most important, it is the natural result of living a vibrant Jewish life.

Women are discovering also the joys of learning together and teaching one another. Our aims may or may not include mastery of the ins and outs of Jewish legal tradition but, whatever our contribution, it must come from a knowledgeable and informed base. Women are insisting, quite properly, that women's Jewish education from elementary school to yeshiva be of the same quality as men's. And—equally important and quite immediate—quality adult education must be available. We must model to our daughters our commitment not only to Jewish practice but also to learning and respecting the tradition of learning, even if we are still questioning it in our own lives. Only in this way can we ensure that richer, deeper women's expression will continue to come forth in the next generation.

Clearly this is an area where much is yet in unformed potential: we cannot foresee the developments in women's spiritual lives over the next few generations. In the process we must be honest to our own pain and difficulties as well as our joys. Most of all, we must continue seeking God as we seek our own growth. Ultimately we will find the "tree of life" that is Torah to be both wise and compassionate. Working from a position committed to a truly Jewish life and to strengthening women can only bring health to our families, our communities, and our land. We will find through this work that God speaking within us and God's speech that has come down to us are not contradictory. "This teaching," said Moses, "is not too hard for you, nor too far. . . . It is very near to you, on your lips and in your heart to do it" (Deut. 30:11, 14). We will be increasingly able to speak this truth. "And God said to Abraham: In all that Sarah tells you, listen to her voice."

There was once a time when, according to the biblical story, it was not good to "listen to her voice." Genesis 3:17: "To Adam He said, 'Because you listened to the voice of your wife and ate of the tree, . . . cursed is the ground because of you; in suffering shall you eat of it all the days of your life." Many feminists have claimed that this story provides a foundation for a negative view of women in Western tradition, because Eve—in Hebrew known as Chava—is to blame for all the troubles of humanity. This is not fair to rabbinic sources, which blame Adam equally or more than Chava.[4] But recent criticisms have gone further, seeing the Garden story as a confrontation between a male God and the symbols of feminine divinity.[5] On the other hand, Carol Meyers has suggested, in a sensitive rereading, that the story is simply an explanation of the human situation as understood in ancient Israel: here is how we came to have the difficulties we have in life—the hard work of tilling the soil and bearing children.[6]

These are all efforts to reconceptualize our human condition: as we retell the stories of the beginnings of humanity, we shape our own lives anew. I suggest a retelling that builds on a gentle midrash. The midrash tells us that the sin of Adam and Chava was not so much disobedience as impatience. Had the two been able to wait a short while, God would have given them the fruit of the Tree of Knowledge. Created on Friday afternoon, if they had just waited a few hours, they could have received from God's own hand the bountiful perfection which God had planned for them on Shabbat.[7] But they listened to the serpent—to the voice which said—go ahead, take it now, you are in control!

Waiting until Shabbat means appreciating what one has now—the whole lovely Garden!—and trusting that God will bless us with whatever we need to satisfy our desires. "You open your hand," says Psalm 145, "and satisfy the desire of every living thing." We work for six days, and then we stop; we step away from the world of grasping and craving. Then God fills our hearts with everything we need. It is said that on Shabbat, we experience, even in this world, a glimpse of that light which, for Adam and Chava, made it possible to see from one end of the world to the other. Had they waited to receive the fruit of the Tree of Knowledge on Shabbat, their sight, their understanding would truly have been God's.

And they would have experienced this vision in perfect union. Shabbat is the time of the union of masculine and feminine, and particularly of the full revelation of the feminine—represented in the Garden by the Tree at the center. Had the couple not been so eager to finish the story quickly, the Shekhinah would have been revealed in her full glory. The union of Adam and Chava would have been perfect, and the world would have been able to continue in the edenic state. Male and female would have reunited, and in this way too they would have truly been like God.

But it did not happen—not then. Ever since, the whole *raison d'etre* of Jewish life is to return the world to the deep knowledge and the unification that would have been the divine gifts to Adam and Chava. The path of return is hinted at by the figures of our history and the work of Jewish life as given in the Torah. It could be said, for example, that Abraham and Sarah symbolically corrected the mistakes of Adam and Chava. They were prophetic figures, and their openness to God's words corrected that yearning for divine knowledge that led to snatching the forbidden fruit. We have Torah study and the work of prayer, exemplified by Channah, to open ourselves to God's direction rather than following only our own forms of knowledge. Abraham and Sarah are known in aggadic lore as great representatives of hospitality: instead of taking food that was to be a divine gift, they gave food to their divine visitors. So too, we have important mitzvot around food: challah, and the whole realm of kashrut. Correlatively, Judaism emphasizes compassionate giving, from hospitality in one's home to charity for all the poor.

So too for the intimate relationship between man and woman, whose balance was upset by the sin in the Garden and afterward must be restored. The figures of Rachel and Leah in their relation to Jacob show how the feminine psyche is to be changed: though they desire to please their husband, they find their own way to God. With women like Yehudit and Tamar, the holiness of sexuality is recalled to us. We have the mitzvah of taharat hamishpocheh which both preserves the holiness of marriage and encourages the independent and interdependent development of husband and wife.

Last but not least, there is Shabbat: the feminine place beyond creation that nurtures all creation, the dimension of inner knowing that Adam and Chava could not reach but that was given finally to the Jewish people at Sinai. After generations of spiritual striving, from Abraham and Sarah to Moses and Zipporah, the gift of Shabbat was made available once more.

These are clues to the path we must take, signposts to a deeper reality. We are at a critical point: the modern world is fraught with difficulties and crises, and we seem to be living in chaos, with little moral and spiritual guidance. We seem to be witnessing the destruction of tradition. Yet the powerful images and archetypes are still there, as is the practical guidance to live a deeply spiritual life. It is no accident that at this moment we as Jewish women are craving exactly what Chava sought: knowledge and wisdom—Torah as divine teaching—and on a personal level, the clear inner sight to continue our tradition and our way of life in the times that lie ahead. When we accept the guidance of the past, when we hear the deep and ancient voices of the women and the feminine in our tradition, we encounter that Torah in ourselves. We can be women seeking wisdom on the foundation that has been established before. We can be women recovering our connection with the deep feminine within, and women speaking with faith and strength out of our discoveries.

Today's clamor and divisiveness is part of that search. It prepares the ground for a new creation, a yet more powerful revelation, when we can once more partake of the Tree of Knowledge and the Tree of Life as it was meant to be. Because we sense this in ourselves, we are all listening to her voice once again.

Notes

PREFACE

1. Rabbi Nathan of Nemirov, *Rabbi Nachman's Wisdom*, trans. Aryeh Kaplan, ed. Zvi Aryeh Rosenfeld (Brooklyn, N.Y.: Breslov Research Institute, 1973), teaching no. 267, p. 397.

PART I

1. Elisabeth Schüssler Fiorenza, "In Search of Women's Heritage," in *Weaving the Visions: New Patterns in Feminist Spirituality*, ed. Judith Plaskow and Carol P. Christ (San Francisco: Harper & Row, 1989; hereafter known as *Visions*), p. 35. Cf. Judith Plaskow, "Jewish Memory from a Feminist Perspective," ibid., 40, who points out that the recovery of history and tradition that pertains to women is especially important in Judaism, where memory, remembering, telling the story, is a religious obligation. This anthology, which includes some of the best pieces of feminist religious writing to date, is highly representative; thus I have cited it frequently.

CHAPTER 1

1. The stereotype of mother is maintained even in recent feminist literature. For example, Catherine Keller, whose otherwise superb critique of Simone de Beauvoir deserves attention, writes of "the strain of picturing any culture in which 'woman's work,' especially mothering, does not circle aimlessly within the confines of life-maintenance." See "Feminism and the Ethic of Inseparability," *Visions*, 261.

    Keller goes on to discuss, and accept, the connection (made by de Beauvoir) between mothers and "mother nature," which supposedly terrified early man; the male had to alienate himself from the woman close to him because she was connected to that terrifying face of nature. I have always been suspicious of the notion that early men feared nature so much more than we do today. I believe that the matter of male-female alienation and power struggles can be better understood in a mode we still find in our own families: the fight for power over children. As in the biblical stories we will examine, women and men had differences over their plans for their children, and the mother's deep power over them—rather than her mysterious connection to nature—could have led him to fear her and plot to outdo her. In addition, of course, there could be deeper psychological connections, such as the male child's ambivalence toward his birth-mother.

2. The balance of early Israelite society is strongly indicated in Carol Meyers's recent work *Discovering Eve: Ancient Israelite Women in Context* (New York: Oxford University Press, 1988).

3. Savina Teubal suggests that Sarah's laughter came from the thought of a priestess of her status having children, rather than from her old age (see discussion of Teubal's work in note 6 below); but in either case, as Teubal agrees, this moment is Sarah's surprise at the ways of this new God she worships. See *Hagar the Egyptian: The Lost Tradition of the Matriarchs* (New York: Harper & Row, 1990), chapter 5.

4. Sarah here is being portrayed as a skeptic—in contrast to Abraham, who passed ten trials in proving his faith in God. Yet Abraham had his moment too; according to some commentaries, he asked God for proof of God's promise that Abraham's descendants would inherit the land, and as a result his descendants had to be slaves in Egypt. The primary source for the negative comment on Abraham is the Talmud (*Nedarim* 32a). Most other commentaries, including Rashi, hold that Abraham was not asking for proof because of a weakness in his faith, but was simply asking by what merit his descendants would deserve it. See the discussion in *Bereishis*, Artscroll Tanach series, vol. 2, ed. Rabbis Nosson Scherman and Meir Zlotowitz (Brooklyn: Mesorah Publications, 1979; hereafter cited as Artscroll *Bereishis*), pp. 517–18.

5. The question has been asked, why did Sarah, a prophetess, not know that the men were angels and that this was a true prophecy? The answer of one commentator is that at this moment her menses came upon her for the first time in many years and clouded her ability to prophesy. While this may sound like a misogynist interpretation, it might fit with the hypothesis (mentioned in note 7) that women of spiritual skill experienced childlessness: perhaps their prophetic ability (or the practices they undertook to develop it) interfered with their menses; or they cultivated solitude at times when they would have been fertile. On the other hand, some writers on women's cycles have suggested that the time of a woman's "dark moon," her menses, might make her more spiritually sensitive. The connection between spiritual sensitivity and menstrual cycles deserves more exploration, both personal and scientific.

6. Ellen M. Umansky, "Creating a Jewish Feminist Theology: Possibilities and Problems," in *Visions*, 196.

7. In a recent work Savina Teubal has tried to develop other hints in order to make the interesting argument that Sarah was indeed a special person in her own right: a priestess from a great family. While a great deal of Teubal's reconstruction of Sarah relies on doubtful hypotheses and some exaggeration of evidence, she is in accord with traditional interpretations in asserting that Sarah is a powerful model of women's spirituality, not just motherhood. See *Sarah the Priestess: The First Matriarch of Genesis* (Athens, Ohio: Swallow Press, 1984).

   Some of her suggestions that may be helpful: Abraham and Sarah left their homeland beyond the Euphrates motivated by a great mission, in which she fully participated. They may well have been from pagan priestly families. The story that Abram's father, Terach, was a seller of idols suggests that he may have been of some priestly status (in those days, one who sold idols was not just running a souvenir stand). If Abram was of priestly descent, Sarai would have been chosen from an equally high family. Moreover, the possibility that Sarah may have been a prophetess-priestess may, Teubal suggests provocatively, be connected to her childlessness. Women in a priestly vocation were not necessarily expected to bear children.

8. Rabbis Scherman and Zlotowitz point out, following the Ramban (Nachmanides) that the Mishkan, and later the Temple, were meant to be replicas of the Jewish home, not vice versa: "Sarah's tent was the Temple upon which God placed His Presence" (Artscroll *Bereishis*, vol. 3, pp. 834–35). This reinforces a point we will make in chapter 2, that woman and Temple represent parallel forms of holiness.

9. This interpretation is from the *N'tziv*; the midrash interprets the verse more in terms of sexual craving: despite the difficulties of pregnancy and labor, a woman's sexual desire will bring her back to union with her husband. See Artscroll *Bereishis*, vol. 1, p. 131.

10. The motif of a woman weeping for her children's fate appears also in the Chicana heritage; see Gloria Anzaldua's comments on La Llorona in "Entering into the Serpent," *Visions*, 81, 85.
11. Artscroll *Bereishis*, vol. 4, pp. 1198–99. In a correlative interpretation, Leah's name, spelled *lamed* (30), *aleph* (1), *hei* (5), adds up to 36; which is twice 18. Eighteen, *chai*, stands for life; double that number can be taken to mean the other world, the next 1ife.

CHAPTER 2

1. The practice of separating the sexes goes back to Temple times and probably earlier. At the Temple a separate "women's court" was provided to guard against anything untoward that might result at the exuberant festival times.
2. This apparent insult is mitigated, in the Chassidic interpretation of the saying, by pointing out that the text says "*the* woman," not *a* woman. One should not pay attention to the woman as woman, but should simply speak with her without regard to her sex. In other words, it is the man's consciousness that is at issue, not the mere fact of gender.
3. This was the law for an adult woman, i.e., a woman over twelve years of age. The rabbis frowned on arranging marriages for girls under twelve, although they could not entirely forbid it since it was sanctioned by Torah tradition. In some cases they required that the marriage be reaffirmed by the woman when she reached adulthood.
4. For a discussion of the variety of views on the dates of King Ahashverus and Mordecai, see Abraham Bloch, *The Biblical and Historical Background of the Jewish Holy Days* (New York: Ktav, 1978).
5. See Mary Gendler, "The Restoration of Vashti," in *The Jewish Woman: New Perspectives*, ed. Elizabeth Koltun (New York: Schocken, 1976), pp. 241–47. While I think the emphasis on Vashti is misplaced, it must be granted that at least one major commentator offers some support for a kinder view of Vashti than the classical midrashim. Rabbi Samson Rafael Hirsch (nineteenth century) points out that Vashti is described in the same terms as Isaac's wife Rivkah: *tovat mareh*, "fair to look on," which is taken by most commentators to connote spiritual rather than physical beauty (which would be *y'fat mareh*). Hirsch suggests that in light of this description we can imagine Vashti as having some spiritual dimension and feelings of decency. For his comment, see Artscroll *Bereishis*, vol. 3, p. 914.
6. Lynn Gottlieb, "The Secret Jew: An Oral Tradition of Women," in *On Being a Jewish Feminist: A Reader* (New York: Schocken, 1983), pp. 271–74.
7. Yehudit was not the first to perform such a feat. A similar motif appears in the story of Yael centuries earlier, in the time of Devorah's judgeship. Yael helped the Israelite general Barak defeat his enemy Sisera, general of Canaanite forces, by offering Sisera refuge then hammering a tent peg through his skull while he slept (Judg. 4:15–24).
8. It is not only in sexuality that this holiness is present; for comparison of Sarah's tent to the Temple, see Chapter 1, note 7.

CHAPTER 3

1. For a brief story of Shulamit, see *Encyclopedia Judaica* (Jerusalem, 1972), vol. 14, pp. 691–92.
2. For some examples, see Sondra Henry and Emily Taitz, *Written out of History* (New York: Bloch Publishing, 1978), and (n.a.) *Sisters of Exile: Sources on the Jewish Woman* (New York: Ichud Habonim Labor Zionist Youth, 1975?).
3. The reference to Hulda is in 2 Kings 22:14; the others are relatively well known. It is notable that the period attributed to the great women of the Bible largely coincides with the premonarchical and early monarchical periods in which Carol Meyers (*Discovering*

Eve, cited above) has identified structures allowing women to have more social power. She does not see the stories of the Matriarchs as helpful in establishing historically the existence of powerful women because of the unreliable nature of the biblical evidence. Nevertheless, evidence from archaeology and some probably premonarchical texts (Song of Songs, possibly the "woman of valor" passage from Proverbs) suggests that this period was one in which women were powerful.

4. Little is known about the spiritual practices of prophets as individuals or in groups. For a discussion of some of the possibilities, see Rabbi Aryeh Kaplan, *Meditation and the Bible* (New York: Samuel Weiser, 1978), part 2.

5. Only in some forms of priesthood are women prominent; but my impression is that those are usually priesthoods that place less emphasis on rituals of animal sacrifice and more on the oracular function of priests or on sexual rituals. More studies need to be done in this area to understand exactly how women's and men's priestly functions differ.

6. Nancy Falk and Rita Gross, *Unspoken Worlds: Women's Religious Lives* (Belmont, Calif.: Wadsworth, 1989), p. 35.

7. Mary Field Belenky et al., *Women's Ways of Knowing: The Development of Self, Voice, and Mind* (New York: Basic Books, 1986), 100–112; on the unconventionality of the women, see p. 104.

8. This does not mean Talmud study is necessarily only "separate knowing," certainly not by comparison with academic learning. The scholar is involved with and cares about the object of study and its practical consequences, which are features of "connected knowing." By comparison to other fields of religious study, however, the area of Talmud is probably the most abstract and "separate," in the sense used by Belenky and her colleagues.

It should be noted also that Belenky et al. do not insist that separate knowing is male and connected knowing female, as this issue has not been sufficiently studied to compare the sexes (p. 103). However, they "believe that connected knowing comes more easily to many women than does separate knowing" (p. 229).

9. Aviva Cantor, "The Lilith Question," in *On Being a Jewish Feminist: A Reader,* ed. Susannah Herschel (New York: Schocken, 1983), pp. 41–50. Cantor's analysis of the development of the Lilith motif is persuasive, and she rightly contrasts the selfish, vengeful portrayal of Lilith with the more selfless model of Esther and others. But, in my opinion, her negative view of altruistic women is inappropriate: as we will see later, feminine spirituality has a relational perspective that naturally includes what might be called "altruism."

10. Adler's criticism, in "The Jew Who Wasn't There," ibid., pp. 14–15, is more to the point: it is not altruism or self-sacrifice per se that makes women's role models less powerful, but their lack of individuation. She goes on to argue that because most women were not learned, their ways of expressing religious commitment were limited. This claim is more questionable, as it puts spirituality only in the hands of the learned.

11. This is confirmed by the conclusions of Belenky et al.: mothers usually speak of childbearing or child rearing as their most powerful learning experiences (*Women's Ways of Knowing,* p. 200).

CHAPTER 4

1. Rabbi Adin Steinsaltz, *Teshuvah: A Guide to the Newly Observant Jew* (New York: Free Press, 1982, Eng. trans. 1987), p. 29.

2. Ibid.

3. For a beautiful and moving description of Shabbat, including its feminine aspect as "queen" or "bride," see Abraham Joshua Heschel, *The Sabbath: Its Meaning for Modern Man* (New York: Farrar, Straus and Giroux, 1951). Heschel's work is still unsurpassed as an evocation of the meaning of Shabbat.

4. Some scholars believe the passage from Proverbs may be premonarchical in origin, i.e., from a historical era when women were more prominent. See Carol Meyers, *Discovering Eve: Ancient Israelite Women in Context* (New York: Oxford University Press, 1988), 179.

5. *Siddur Tehillat Hashem*, Nusach Ha-Ari Zal, according to the text of Rabbi Schneur Zalman of Liadi, trans. Nissen Mangel (Brooklyn: Merkos L'Inyonei Chinuch, 1978), pp. 133, 134.

6. Ibid., pp. 140, 146. The translation from the Amidah is usually given as "thereon," so it is not immediately recognizable as the feminine "on her." The special kabbalistic titles used here refer to various manifestations of the divine energies, one feminine and two masculine, respectively.

7. For a history, see Rafael Patai's *The Hebrew Goddess* (New York: Avon Books, 1967). Some feminists have complained that the idea of the Shekhinah is not particularly useful, since it was not originally feminine and, even when it has been, it has not empowered women but has "only supported the male-centered vision." See Marcia Falk, "Notes on Composing New Blessings: Toward a Feminist-Jewish Reconstruction of Prayer," *Visions*, pp.129–30. I frankly do not find the argument convincing, simply because many women in my experience do find the Shekhinah image viable and inspiring. The hierarchical polarization Falk finds objectionable in the kabbalistic interpretation of the Shekhinah has to do with the transcendent-immanent dichotomy, which we will discuss more fully in chapter 7.

8. Some have taken this metaphor as expressing a negative valuation of woman. See, for example, Rosemary Radford Reuther, "Sexism and God-Language," in *Visions*, 152. She claims that God, the "groom," is possessive, jealous, and judgmental; while humankind, the "bride," is his female servant. She takes this to be a reversal of the ancient Near Eastern portrayal of the Queen of Heaven with her male consort. On the level of mythology, this certainly appears to be the same motif with genders reversed. But to portray the Jewish version as wholly negative is unfounded. True, as she notes, the prophet Hosea and others use the motif to accuse Israel of harlotry, being the unfaithful wife, when the people worship other gods. She reads it as carrying a negative stereotype of women, based on a double standard that dominates Bible and rabbinic tradition; but the Queen of Heaven in other traditions accuses her male lovers of similar unfaithfulness. Sexism is not the issue here, but rather the rhetorical use of a metaphor.

  In Judaism, other uses of the metaphor are quite positive. God's redemption of his "bride," Israel, from slavery in Egypt in response to their cries echoes Isis's search for Tammuz in the underworld but with a great sense of compassion added: God performs an act of love not dependent on Israel's merit. And while Israel is often presented as the weaker partner compared to the "king," their love, as in the *Shir HaShirim* (Song of Songs), is profound and moving on both sides. In rabbinic presentations of the "unfaithful wife" motif (e.g., in interpreting the story of the golden calf) the fault on Israel's side is clearly understood as a general human flaw, not a sin of woman. Indeed, women are specifically exempted from complicity in it. The picture, in short, is much more complex than Reuther allows in her brief allusion to this metaphor.

9. Carol Meyers, *Discovering Eve*, pp. 178–79, discusses the powerful female images in the song. For Waskow's comment, see "Feminist Judaism: Restoration of the Moon," in *On Being a Jewish Feminist: A Reader* ed. Susannah Herschel (New York: Schocken, 1983), p. 264.

10. This was a time of mourning in some of the other traditions of the ancient Near East, particularly those connected with nature deities. Midsummer, when the land begins to dry out and the grass to turn brown, was associated with the disappearance of the forces of fertility. Mythologically, the male consort of the great goddess died, and she went into mourning for him. The pagan idea as such had no place in Judaism: we find a prophet criticizing those "women mourning for Tammuz," the female devotees who identified with the goddess's sadness. But the parallel with the seasonal forces of nature is clear.

11. The phrase is from Masha Zweibel, "Jewish Women Shaped History," in *The Modern Jewish Woman: A Unique Perspective,* ed. Raizel Schnall Friedfertig and Freyda Schapiro (Brooklyn: Lubavitch Educational Foundation, 1981), p. 152.

12. It is no accident either that other cultures mark this same time of year—late winter to early spring—with great costume events, parades, and "calling of the spirits." We need only think of Chinese New Year, or Carnival and Mardi Gras in Roman Catholic regions. The seasonal significance is the emergence of the spirits from their hidden winter habitations, before the trees and crops begin to emerge.

CHAPTER 5

1. One of the most passionate criticisms is that of Rachel Adler, in her article "The Jew Who Wasn't There," in *On Being a Jewish Feminist: A Reader* (New York: Schocken, 1983). She claimed that women's mitzvot often demanded masochistic self-sacrifice, and found it "most damaging that the woman's meager *mitzvot* are, for the most part, closely connected to some physical goal or object . . . without any independent spiritual life to counterbalance the materialism of her existence" (p. 15). However, other feminist thinkers hold that the physical connection is a valuable part of women's spirituality. For further discussion, see chapter 7.

2. Caroline Walker Bynum, *Holy Feast and Holy Fast: The Significance of Food to Medieval Women* (Berkeley: University of California Press, 1987), p. 190. Bynum's fascinating study shows clearly how food imagery was central to the spirituality of many medieval Christian women.

3. Michel Abehsera, *Cooking with Care and Purpose* (Brooklyn: Swan House Publishing, 1978), p. 21.

4. Kim Chernin, *Reinventing Eve: Modern Woman in Search of Herself* (New York: Harper & Row, 1987).

5. In this connection, Jacob Neusner's excellent discussion of the grace after meals is well worth examining; see *The Enchantments of Judaism: Rites of Transformation from Birth Through Death* (New York: Basic Books, 1987), chapter 2.

6. In Judaism we may note that Rivkah, Rachel, and Zipporah were all connected with wells. Eliezer met Rivkah at a well and brought her home to Isaac; Jacob and Moses each met their future wives at wells.

7. Rabbi Aryeh Kaplan, *The Waters of Eden: An Exploration of the Concept of Mikvah Renewal and Rebirth,* 2d ed. (New York: National Conference of Synagogue Youth, 1982).

8. Much mystical teaching for men focuses on inwardness as well; but we should recognize that this is an adaptation of metaphors from the feminine side of the psyche. As Chassidus explicitly teaches, men must develop their receptive, "feminine" side. Classically, the masculine metaphors of spirituality are more outer-directed: the prophet on the mountain, the hero on his quest, the thaumaturge ascending to higher spheres.

9. Heschel, *The Sabbath: Its Meaning for Modern Man* (New York: Farrar, Straus and Giroux, 1951) p. 109, n. 1. Heschel notes that "between . . . and" is a Hebrew expression for the intimacy of husband and wife (cf. *Nedarim* 79b). The entire expression is, "between Me and Israel it is a sign for Israel *l'olam* [forever]." Heschel observes that *l'olam* could be vocalized *l'alem,* "to be kept as a secret" (*Bezah* 16a).

10. Specifically, the cup symbolizes the womb. See, e.g., E. S. Drower, "Evergreen Elijah," ed. Jorunn Jacobson Buckley, in *Approaches to Ancient Judaism* 6, ed. Jacob Neusner and Ernest S. Frerichs (Scholars Press: Brown Judaic Studies 192, 1989), p. 20. It is no accident, then, that many have the custom of pouring the cup before reciting "Woman of Valor."

11. Ibid., pp. 66, 74, 88.

CHAPTER 6

1. For example, the early rebbes of Chabad-Lubavitch encouraged women to learn privately; this was in the early nineteenth century. Separate schools for women came later, after the turn of the present century. We should remember also that even in secular culture it was not customary for women to have advanced education similar to that of men until the late nineteenth and early twentieth centuries. For an interesting commentary on the shifts in attitudes toward women's education, see Deborah Weissman, "Bais Yaakov: A Historical Model for Jewish Feminists," in *The Jewish Woman: New Perspectives*, ed. Elizabeth Koltun (New York: Schocken, 1976).

2. Midrash includes biblical exegesis and sermons on specific books of the Bible and is a rich source of stories and homilies, largely from mishnaic and talmudic periods. Aggadah is the term for the larger body of nonhalachic tradition (narratives, explanations, ethical maxims and advice), extending from midrash down to the present. Musar is modern (post-eighteenth century) ethics; kabbalah is the mystical tradition; and Chassidus is a modern tradition that uses mystical concepts to help the ordinary person understand the purpose and method of Torah and mitzvot. Chumash comprises the Five Books of Moses, while Tanach, the Hebrew Bible, includes the Five plus the "Prophets," historical and prophetic literature, and the "Writings," the wisdom literature and later biblical writings.

3. This follows Rabbi Adin Steinsaltz's summary in *Teshuvah: A Guide to the Newly Observant Jew* (New York: Free Press, 1982; Eng. trans. 1987), p. 147. He notes there also, citing the authority of the Rambam (Maimonides), that even though a woman "is not commanded to study Torah, to the extent that she is inclined to do so she receives a reward." It might be mentioned as well that because she is obligated in the mitzvah of *chinuch* (education of children), a mother, or a woman who teaches children, often has to learn areas of Torah not normally required of a woman.

4. Rabbi Adin Steinsaltz, *The Long Shorter Way: Discourses on Chasidic Thought*, ed. and trans. Yehuda Hanegbi (Northvale, N.J.: Jason Aronson, 1988), pp. 147, 148–49. My discussion of Torah study is partly indebted to his excellent explanation in chapter 23. This work is based on Rabbi Steinsaltz's lectures on the first portion of the *Tanya* (the *Likutei Amarim*) by Rabbi Schneur Zalman of Liadi, founder of Chabad-Lubavitch, known as the Alter Rebbe.

5. Jacob Neusner has provided a good description of how words create worlds: how in reciting words of ritual our imagination transforms us into something other than what we usually are. In my view, prayer begins there and, ideally, goes further, to an experience beyond the conscious workings of imagination. For his discussion, see *The Enchantments of Judaism: Rites of Transformation from Birth through Death* (New York: Basic Books, 1987), prologue and passim.

6. On Shabbat, holidays, and days when the Torah is read, there are additions: the Torah reading and Musaf (an additional Amidah). Various interpolations are made in the prayers, appropriate to the particular day.

7. Women are obligated to pray twice a day. While there are differences of opinion as to what should constitute women's prayer, most authorities agree that highest priority should be given to the Shemoneh Esreh of Shacharit and Mincha. In addition, women often take on the saying of Shema morning and evening. Men pray three times a day because the evening saying of Shema was developed into a third service of prayer, including an additional Shemoneh Esreh. While this was not a Torah obligation, it became so universal a custom that the rabbis established it as an additional obligatory service for men.

8. For a few examples, see Marcia Cohn Spiegel, ed., *Women Speak to God: The Prayers and Poems of Jewish Women* (San Diego: Women's Institute for Continuing Jewish Education, 1987); and Chava Weissler, "Voices from the Heart: Women's Devotional Prayers," in *The Jewish Almanac*, ed. Richard Siegel and Carl Rheins (New York: Bantam Books, 1980),

541–45. Women's work in liturgical and interpretive areas is discussed by Sondra Henry and Emily Taitz, *Written Out of History* (New York: Bloch Publishing, 1978).
9. Rabbi Aryeh Kaplan, *Meditation and the Bible* (New York: Samuel Weiser, 1978) p. 2.

PART III

1. Leading examples include the very important books by Carol Gilligan, *In a Different Voice*, which one now finds cited in almost every feminist study, and Mary Belenky et al., *Women's Ways of Knowing* (cited in chap. 3, n. 8). Historical studies of women's self-expression also lend support to this stance, for example, Caroline Walker Bynum's *Holy Feast and Holy Fast: The Significance of Food to Medieval Women* (Berkeley: University of California Press, 1987).

   Of course, Jungian studies have held for some time to a theory that claims significant personality differences between the sexes; see the classics by Erich Neumann, *The Great Mother* (Princeton University Press, 1955); M. Esther Harding, *Women's Mysteries, Ancient and Modern*, 2d ed. (New York: Harper & Row, 1978); Irene Castillejo, *Knowing Woman* (New York: Harper & Row, 1974); and a reworking of Jungian and Gestalt theory, Jennifer Barker Woolger and Roger J. Woolger, *The Goddess Within* (New York: Fawcett Columbine, 1989). In light of the problems of dualism in Western thought that we will discuss in chapter 7, readers should note Naomi R. Goldenberg's critique of Jungian theory: "Archetypal Theory and the Separation of Mind and Body," in *Visions*, pp. 244–55.
2. A number of articles in Plaskow and Christ, eds., *Visions*, take this perspective, but probably the most influential recent statement is that of Riane Eisler in *The Chalice and the Blade: Our History, Our Future* (San Francisco: Harper & Row, 1987).

CHAPTER 7

1. For an excellent overview of Jewish feminist issues, see Judith Plaskow, *Standing Again at Sinai* (N.Y.: Harper & Row, 1990).
2. Simone de Beauvoir, *The Second Sex*, trans. H. M. Parshley (New York: Vintage Books, 1974).
3. Catherine Keller, "Feminism and the Ethic of Inseparability," *Visions*, pp. 259.
4. Rosemary Radford Reuther, "Sexism and God-Language," *Visions*, pp. 160–61.
5. Keller, "Inseparability," pp. 262–64.
6. Christ, "Rethinking Theology and Nature," *Visions*, p. 323. In much of this article she is criticizing the modern theologian Gordon Kaufman.
7. Ibid., p. 322.
8. Plaskow and Christ, "Self in Relation," *Visions*, p. 173.
9. Beverly Wildung Harrison, "The Power of Anger in the Work of Love," *Visions*, p. 221.
10. Ibid., p. 220.
11. Christ, "Rethinking," pp. 319, 322.
12. Harrison, "Work of Love," pp. 218–19. A yet more radical view is represented by Audre Lourde in her article "Uses of the Erotic," *Visions*, pp. 208–13. Claiming that the erotic – by which she means shared pleasurable, joyful feelings representing "the lifeforce of women"– is the basis of true knowledge, she holds that "It feels right to me," understood deeply, not superficially, is a sound foundation. Understanding is its "handmaiden," to "clarify that knowledge, deeply born." By separating feeling from spirituality, she argues that the Euroamerican tradition has reduced the spiritual "to a world of flattened affect, a world of the ascetic who aspires to feel nothing. But . . . the ascetic position is one of the highest fear, the gravest immobility . . . not of self-discipline but of self-abnegation."

13. Harrison, "Work of Love," p. 215. She continues, "A theology that overvalues static or passive qualities as 'holy,' that equates spirituality with noninvolvement and contemplation, that views the activity of sustaining daily life as mundane and unimportant religiously, such a theology *could not have been formulated by women.*" The balance that, I will suggest, is exemplified in Jewish thought on these matters exists precisely because women's participation is important in Jewish life.

14. Abraham Isaac Kook, "Fragments of Light: A View as to the Reasons for the Commandments," in *Lights*, p. 313.

15. Rosemary Reuther is aware of this quality when she comments that beyond the "sacred marriage" motif, which she sees as oppressive, the relation between God and Israel is one of liberation, leading away from oppression and patriarchy ("Sexism and God-Language," *Visions*, p. 155). This is, of course, one of the foundations of contemporary "liberation theology," but feminists have criticized male versions of this theology.

16. The rabbis were concerned about this question and asked by what merit the Israelites were redeemed. One answer was "in the merit of the women," as discussed on p. 113; another was that the people had not completely given up their heritage—they kept their Jewish names and the Hebrew language. Also, there was the merit of their fathers Abraham, Isaac, and Jacob that God remembered. But these are attempts to justify in terms of a (masculine) morality of rights and merits an act that was regarded as essentially unfathomable.

17. Tradition makes this clear: God told Abraham his descendants would be slaves for 400 years, but the actual term of slavery was 210 years. God reduced the term that would have been required by strict justice.

18. Harrison, "Work of Love," p. 220.

19. Keller, "Inseparability," p. 264.

20. For an interesting and highly readable excursion in Jewish views of the body and its organs, see Moshe Goldberger, *Singing Hashem's Praises: Lessons from the Organs of the Body* (Brooklyn: Graphi Text, 1987).

21. Already with the growing interest in kabbalah and Chassidus, some of the immanentalist perspective is entering into the Jewish mainstream and affecting men as well as women. But we must be cautious: the Greek philosophical influence on this aspect of tradition is quite strong. The devaluation of body and sensuality creates an enormous block for many women and could lead to subversion of feminine ideals.

CHAPTER 8

1. The traditional objections to women's entering the rabbinate are probably well known to most readers, but it will be helpful to reiterate them here. First it should be noted that the reasons do not include women's inferiority of intellect (or anything else) or a prohibition on women's learning. Women with the desire to learn have often done so in the past and in a few instances have been regarded by their peers as sufficiently accomplished to *poskin*—that is, to hand down halachic decisions. Such women were consulted by men, including other rabbis, as well as women. This, however, has been the rare case.

Still, there would not be a problem (theoretically, at least) with women becoming rabbis if it were not also the case that other tasks, besides giving halachic decisions, have become attached to the rabbi's role. Women are not permitted to lead a mixed group in prayer or to be official witnesses of documents, for example, marriage contracts. These would not necessarily preclude a woman's being a rabbi even within current halacha. She could obtain other witnesses for any document, and the congregation could appoint a chazzan to lead the congregation in her place. But the awkwardness of these accommodations, and the obvious displacement of a leader from her role in certain instances, create what would likely be an uncomfortable situation.

A woman's being a chazzan, or leader of worship, faces more difficulty. Women do not lead mixed worship services because they are not under the same obligations as men in prayer. While obligated to pray, women are exempt from praying at fixed times; and most rabbinic opinions hold that we are not obligated to daven the entire service. Therefore, a woman can lead other women in prayer but not a mixed group. Further, a woman's solo singing voice is considered potentially distracting to men's concentration on their prayers.

2. Some women accept the separation of sexes but have difficulty with what they experience as women's distance—physically and thus also symbolically—from the Torah scrolls themselves. Different orthodox congregations have attempted to resolve this by varying spatial arrangements, or even, though many halachic authorities question this, by permitting women's minyans to read from the Torah. The issue is not yet resolved. It is important to understand that what is at stake is women's deep experience of love for the Torah and a search for an appropriate expression of that without necessarily disrupting the male-female dynamic of the traditional synagogue.

3. The Beruria story has been treated, most recently by Rachel Adler (see "The Virgin and the Brothel," *Tikkun* vol. 3 [Nov–Dec 1988], pp. 28ff.), as one in which a scholarly woman eventually ended up being suspected and derided. The story of her supposed downfall (her falling victim to a seduction plot by a rabbinical student), is, however, from a much later era of tradition than the rest of her story and may not have much basis in fact. Even if it is true, however, it reveals more about male jealousy than about Beruria herself. There is no doubt she was fully accepted as a scholar and teacher in her time.

4. For example, Radak and Ibn Ezra point out that the text says he was *imah*, "at one with her"—i.e., not hopelessly tempted or deceived; and the Abarbanel holds that Adam was actually the prime sinner because he had been the prime recipient of the command. See Artscroll *Bereishis*, vol. 1, pp. 120, 131.

5. See Riane Eisler, *The Chalice and the Blade: Our History, Our Future* (New York: Harper & Row, 1987), and Kim Chernin, *Reinventing Eve: Modern Woman in Search of Herself* (New York: Harper & Row, 1987). These writers suggest that Chava was being offered feminine sources of knowledge (the tree of knowledge, with the serpent symbolizing an oracle of the feminine deity), and the patriarchal deity was punishing her and her husband for seeking this knowledge. While this is an interesting re-reading of the text, it does not explain Adam's role or any of the subtleties of the story (e.g., tree of knowledge vs. tree of life, the punishment of tilling the ground). Moreover, the harshness of the male / female confrontation depends largely on understanding Chava's punishment as submission to a patriarchal husband—a reading which, after the work of Carole Meyers, can no longer be sustained. The Garden story contains many fascinating motifs and has been the subject of tomes of interpretation in Jewish writings alone, from the Talmud to the Zohar and on into modern writings. It deserves a fuller analysis than we can undertake here.

6. See Meyers's retranslation and explication of the story and the so-called curse, really a poetic oracle to Chava, in *Discovering Eve: Ancient Israelite Women in Context* (New York: Oxford University Press, 1988), pp. 95–121.

7. See "An Overview: Adam and Sin," Artscroll *Bereishis*, vol. 1, p. 18. Rabbi Aryeh Kaplan comments on The Bahir, an early kabbalistic text, that Adam "did not attain his main aspect of soul . . . until the first Sabbath. . . . His main sin was the fact that he did not wait, but ate of it [the Tree] on the sixth day." See *The Bahir* (New York: Samuel Weiser, 1979), p. 176.